W9-BAK-318

FROM OATH
TO ACTION

Dear Sandy,

    Yay! I already love working together. Can't wait to see what we create!

    Onward!

FROM OATH TO ACTION

Simple
Acts *of*
Courage
to Rebuild
American Democracy

JEFF EDELSTEIN

Copyright © 2016 by Jeff Edelstein

All rights reserved
Printed in the United States of America
First Edition

No part of this book may be reproduced in any manner
whatsoever, stored in a retrieval system, or transmitted in any form
or by any means, electronic, mechanical, photocopying, recording,
or otherwise, without prior written permission of the publisher,
except in the case of brief quotations embodied in critical articles
or reviews. Requests for permission should be directed to
info@fromoathtoaction.com.

To my father, Bernard Edelstein
He ran his race with kindness, generosity and courage
1926 – 2010

Acknowledgments

I am grateful to the many people who helped in the creation of this book, each of whom contributed in his or her own way, whether providing ideas, insights, editing, encouragement, discussion, debate or other forms of assistance. I would like to particularly thank Eric Rounds, Paul Haley, Adam Eilenberg, Ona Ferguson, Donna Giroux, Dave Weinberg, Matt Craig, Fred Dillon, Ishwari Sollohub, Susan Edelstein, Sue Inches, Chris Jonas, Heather Chandler, Jan Kearce, Audrey Knapp, Harold Pachios, John Braman, Ed Radtke, Ray Raphael, Jill Maxi Schreibman, and most especially my mother, Marjorie Edelstein, for inspiring me to persevere, and Liz Farmer for her insights, support, and encouragement.

CONTENTS

PREFACE

My goal in publishing *From Oath to Action* is to offer a new vision of what political leadership is, or could be, in the 21st century. At a time when so many Americans seem fed up with our political system, I wish to provide a ray of hope. We *can* rebuild our democracy. The path I suggest may take time, but it just might take us where we need to go.

From Oath to Action presents a rare political message. Put aside the exposés, screeds, and rants. They just feed the flames of partisanship. Put aside the manifestos seeking constitutional reform. They are mere pipedreams. This doesn't mean we don't need to fix our political institutions. We do. But institutions change only when the people in them change and most people change just one step at a time. Rather than cause for despair, however, that fact should be cause for hope. Because one step at a time is achievable.

Many who pursue public office have their hearts in the right place. They start out intending to do what's right. Along the way, however, the system wears them down. Eventually their courage—their willingness to take on the system—gets lost.

But within nearly every politician, I believe, a spark of courage still burns. Courage to stop and listen. Courage to admit they don't know all the answers. Courage to take action, even at the risk of failure.

What we, the American people, can do—what we must do—is to help re-ignite those sparks. Let us call for our leaders to rebuild our democracy, *one simple act of courage at a time.*

In the pages ahead, I suggest twelve such acts. They all have one thing in common: they require no new laws, no changes to the constitution, no fixing of congressional rules. Any politician can undertake any one of these acts any time they choose. All it takes is a little courage.

By the time you've finished this book, I hope you will be inspired to spread its message: share these ideas with friends, family and colleagues; contact your members of Congress; speak out publicly; or take whatever action suits you best. And I encourage you to offer up your own ideas for acts of courage to rebuild our democracy at www.fromoathtoaction.com. We're all in this together. I invite you to join this endeavor.

INTRODUCTION

American democracy sorely needs repair. Whether we live in a red state or blue state, whether we consider ourselves a liberal, conservative, moderate, Tea Partier, Democrat, Republican, Green, or Independent, few among us would deny that our democracy is on the skids.

Many of us feel frightened, angry, or helpless as our nation's prosperity and security slip away amid global forces that our government appears unprepared, unwilling, or unable to confront. We despair at the warring ideologies reducing American politics to an irrelevant sideshow as the world moves on without us.

At the same time, many of us are conflicted. Despite a growing sense that our country is on the wrong track, we are still—at least for the time being—the wealthiest, most powerful, and most free nation in the world. We fear for our future, but are reluctant to rock the boat that has kept us comfortably afloat. We long for change, but not too quickly. We prefer to be arm-chair revolutionaries.

But we cannot ignore the fact that our democracy no longer works. Witness the government shutdowns, the runaway national debt, congressional gridlock, the "legal corruption" of campaign donations, and an electoral system that seemingly guarantees members of Congress a seat for life.

Meanwhile, around the globe, we witness the "rise of the rest," as described by Fareed Zakaria in *The Post-American World*: the emergence of China, India, Russia, Brazil and other countries as major players on the world stage—economically, militarily, and politically. Zakaria observes that if America is to retain any leadership at all, it will be as "first among equals," a role we are unaccustomed to playing.

FROM OATH TO ACTION

Yet even retaining that role is an uncertain proposition. While governments around the world have adapted to the needs of the 21st century, the structures of American democracy remain mired in the late 1700's world of horse carriages, knee breeches, and powdered wigs. What had been our strength—the resistance of our democratic system to capricious change—is proving to be our downfall as it prevents us from responding to today's rapidly changing world.

Again quoting Zakaria: "[The U.S.] has developed a highly dysfunctional politics. An antiquated and overly rigid political system to begin with—about 225 years old—has been captured by money, special interests, a sensationalist media, and ideological attack groups. The result is ceaseless, virulent debate about trivia—politics as theater—and very little substance, compromise and action…A "can-do" country is now saddled with a "do-nothing" political process, designed for partisan battle rather than problem-solving…those who advocate sensible solutions and compromise legislation find themselves marginalized by their party's leadership, losing funds from special-interest groups, and being constantly attacked by their "side" on television and radio. The system provides greater incentives to stand firm and go back and tell your team that you refused to bow to the enemy. It's great for fundraising, but it's terrible for governing."

But how can we fix a broken political system that has a built-in resistance to repair? Constitutional reform is nearly impossible; our Constitution is arguably the world's most difficult to change. Witness how, in the nearly 250 years since the ratification of the Constitution, only three amendments—the Twelfth, Seventeenth, and Twenty-Second—might be said to have made substantive changes to our government's structure. Consider the Electoral College, America's convoluted—and many would say

INTRODUCTION

undemocratic—method of electing the president, a method that an overwhelming majority of Americans oppose. Despite over 700 bills seeking to change or abolish the current system through constitutional reform that have been introduced in Congress over the past two centuries, not a single one has made it through to passage.

Attempts to reform our democracy through legislation, while easier to accomplish, have proven similarly futile. Those in power are loath to change the system that has benefited them so greatly, and in those rare instances when they have—such as campaign finance laws—ways to work around those reforms have quickly been found.

What about simply electing better leaders? Again, we face daunting obstacles. While we decry the partisan bickering that is destroying our democracy and yearn for leaders with the courage to negotiate common-sense solutions, an unfortunate convergence of forces—the primary system, congressional redistricting, the capture of the political process by moneyed interests, and the 24/7 spotlight of media and digital coverage—has conspired to offer us increasingly extremist and unyielding candidates.

But this does not mean there is no hope. It simply means that if we aspire to restore the greatness of American democracy—to reclaim this exceptional experiment in government "of the people, by the people, for the people"—then we must do so with our feet planted firmly in the soil of reality. We are no longer the upstart nation of more than two centuries ago. The founders overthrew a system of government so egregious it left them little choice but to create a wholly new form of government. Our generation's calling is different. The fabric of our democracy may be tattered and frayed, but it is not irreparably torn. Our task is to mend it, not replace it entirely.

FROM OATH TO ACTION

For too long, reformers have focused on fixing the institutions of government, while neglecting the people—our elected leaders—at the heart of them. And therein is where hope resides. Despite the many ways Americans may differ, we all seek the same traits in our leaders: courage, compassion, innovation, integrity, accountability, fairness, wisdom, and a commitment to working together to solve America's problems. And while our system of democracy may not always serve to elect such leaders, those we do elect can learn these traits. The central message of *From Oath to Action* to our leaders is this: "keep your partisanship, battle over the issues, but also commit to at least one act to rebuild a functioning democracy."

Isn't that the American way? Our democracy grew strong and our nation has prospered because we have valued the power of individual action. America has always been a place where individuals can make a difference, whether rising from commonplace roots to become the president of the United States or starting a company that changes the world. The very idea of representative democracy is that individuals in office will do what's right, not just what's convenient. That notion may, at times, seem lost in Washington, but it can be brought back to life.

From Oath to Action is the launching of a political insurgency, a campaign to infiltrate the system, one politician at a time. What starts as a trickle will build to an unstoppable flood. The central tenets of this campaign are these: that the ideals of accountability, innovation, courage and the like are hollow notions without the actions that further them; that these ideals belong not to Democrats, Republicans, or members of any other party, but are the common aspiration of all; that people are endowed with both virtue and vice, both of which can be harnessed for the public good.

INTRODUCTION

If America is to thrive in a world that has emerged from the black-and-white simplicity of the Cold War into a complex geopolitical landscape, then our politics need to move beyond "either-or" thinking. We need bipartisanship *and* partisanship; collaboration *and* competition; innovation *and* tradition. We need to transform our democracy *and* retain our Constitution. We need ideologies *and* ideals.

Most of all, we need our leaders in Washington to take not just the oath of office, but an oath to action. To break the gridlock in Washington, we need them to undertake individual acts that will begin to restore the functioning of the very institutions of government itself: the House of Representatives, the Senate, and the presidency.

In the pages that follow, I describe twelve simple acts of courage for members of Congress and the president to undertake. *From Oath to Action* does not call upon any one leader to undertake all of these. As a start, just one act will suffice. One act of honor, understanding, innovation, teamwork, fairness, accountability, learning, responsibility, honesty, integrity, or wisdom.

Every journey begins with a single step. Let us begin the rebuilding of our democracy. Let us move from oath to action.

THE IMPROBABILITY OF CONSTITUTIONAL REFORM

The purpose of this brief chapter is to put to rest any lingering questions about this book's premise: that the path to fixing our democracy rests upon individual acts of courage, rather than attempting constitutional reform. Some readers might ask: Why not change the Constitution to eliminate the Electoral College? Establish term limits for members of Congress? Make Senate representation proportional to population? Require Congress to pass a balanced budget? Restrain the role of money in politics?

I am not arguing against constitutional reform, only against the idea that it can be accomplished soon enough or go far enough. By examining the (somewhat peculiar) circumstances of the Constitution's creation, the rise of political parties shortly thereafter, and the history of constitutional reform efforts, I hope to help the reader understand why such reform, at this time, is a near impossibility. On the other hand, changing the way politicians behave—one simple act at a time—is achievable, will produce results quicker, and is, in fact, a necessary precursor to any attempts at constitutional reform.

The reality is that the framers, intentionally or not, erected nearly impenetrable barriers to amending the Constitution. We may as well try to change the law of gravity. In the more than two centuries since the ratification of the Constitution, over 11,000 amendments have been introduced in Congress. Only 33 have been passed and only 27 of those have been ratified by the states. And most of these amendments, while important to a free society, either safeguarded individual rights or made minor technical changes to our democratic system, but did little or nothing to address the structural deficiencies that are becoming increasingly apparent.

Even the three constitutional amendments that *did* make structural changes were limited: the Twelfth Amendment fixed a flaw in the presidential electoral system, but left intact the widely-despised Electoral College; the Seventeenth Amendment gave the citizenry the right to elect U.S. Senators, but did nothing to address the fundamental inequity of the two-Senators-per-state framework; and the Twenty-Second Amendment—setting term limits for the presidency—merely codified a 150-year old unwritten rule that had been temporarily breached.

We must remember that the Constitution does two things: it dictates the structures of our government and safeguards the rights of the citizens. The framers focused nearly entirely on the former by setting up the three branches of government, establishing qualifications for elected office, and such. Nearly all the rights of citizens came later—in the ten amendments comprising the Bill of Rights and in most of the subsequent seventeen amendments.

I am not saying that any of the amendments are unimportant. Far from it. The actions to abolish slavery, establish freedom of religion, of speech, of the press, and the like, have been instrumental in securing the "unalienable rights," as described in the Declaration of Independence, of "life, liberty, and the pursuit of happiness." But when it comes to managing the affairs of the nation, it is the structures of our government, not our rights, that matter most. Our government can protect all our rights in the world, yet still put the nation deeper into debt, send us into ill-fated wars, and allow our roads, bridges and schools to fall into disrepair.

To understand why changing the Constitution is so difficult, we need to briefly examine its history. What many of us remember from school—that the colonists freed themselves from the British and wrote a Constitution to form the new nation's government—is at best an oversimplification, and at worst, simply inaccurate.

The so-called Constitutional Convention was not convened to write a Constitution at all, but rather to revise the existing Articles of Confederation. But the delegates to the convention—those who we call the framers of the Constitution—rejected that charge. They decided that the Articles of Confederation were beyond repair and should be replaced entirely, and what's more, that the drafting of the new document should be done in secret. Four months later, they presented their new Constitution, decreeing that no changes could be made until the states formally adopted the document. So despite the Constitution beginning with the words "We, the people" the fact is that the "people" of the thirteen states had little role in its creation.

An interesting perspective on the Constitution is provided by David Hendrickson in *Peace Pact: The Lost World of the American Founding*. Hendrickson describes the Constitution not so much as a guiding document for a new nation, but as a "peace pact" among thirteen sovereign nations concerned primarily with preventing hostilities among themselves; ensuring the free flow of commerce; and maintaining a military alliance to repel foreign invaders and suppress rebellions.

Hendrickson's view makes sense when one considers that from the time the Pilgrims landed at Plymouth Rock until the Constitutional Convention, North America was a frequent battleground for wars between England, France, Holland, Spain, and the native tribes, not to mention the Revolutionary War between the colonists and the British. In the 1700s alone, there was the Queen Anne's War (1702 – 1713), King George's War (1744 – 1748), the French and Indian war (1754 – 1763), the War of the Regulation (1764 – 1771) and the Revolutionary War (1775 – 1783).

With such continual eruption of warfare, would it be unexpected for the founders to be seeking a pre-emptive "peace treaty?" Hendrickson argues that threats of rebellion within the states, conflicts between the states, and continuing tensions with England drove the desire to revise the Articles of Confederation, far more than any aspirations for "nation-building."

Indeed, the notion that the inhabitants of the thirteen states generally considered themselves citizens of a single nation is mistaken. Consider life on the North American continent in the late 1700s. Inhabitants of the different states had little to do with one other, going about their lives within tight circles and rarely venturing beyond their villages and towns. Just getting from New York to Philadelphia—barely 100 miles apart—took up to three days by stagecoach. Each state had its own constitution and its own government. It was not unusual for Americans of this period to refer to their home state as their "country."

By viewing the Constitution as a treaty among sovereign states, we can better understand why the framers gave the citizenry no direct rights to propose, approve, or reject amendments, reserving those powers to the Congress and the state governments alone. And even the states' authority—absent the highly unlikely scenario of a second constitutional convention—is limited to ratifying or rejecting amendments, not proposing them. Thus, the reality is that Congress holds the keys to constitutional reform. The Constitution can only be changed if first, a member of Congress proposes an amendment, and then second—most important—if it is approved by two-thirds votes of both the Senate and the House of Representatives. Only then does the amendment go to the states, requiring approval by three-quarters of the states to be enacted.

But still you might ask why that makes constitutional reform so difficult. After all, over 11,000 amendments have been proposed by members of Congress since the Constitution was ratified. Why have only 33 been passed?

The first reason is the existence of political parties which, although non-existent when the Constitution was written, arose soon after. Constitutional amendments—like much other legislation—tend to become partisan issues. That might not pose a problem if either party held the two-thirds majority in both houses of Congress needed to pass an amendment. But such circumstances have occurred in only 6 out of the past 150 years, and not at all in nearly the past 50 years. Indeed, 40 years have passed since either party has held a two-thirds majority in even one house of Congress. This might explain why the last amendment to the Constitution (a fairly non-controversial change lowering the voting age to 18) was passed by Congress nearly 50 years ago, the longest such period since the first half of the 19th century. Given today's extreme state of partisanship that prevents Congress from accomplishing even the most mundane things, do we really expect its members to cross party lines to vote for a constitutional amendment?

A second reason—particularly relevant to attempts to eliminate or reform the Electoral College, one of the most reviled parts of the Constitution—is the structure of the Senate, which gives each state two Senators regardless of population. The Senators from the smaller states tend to oppose any threats to the disproportionate power the Electoral College provides their states. While the thirty-four Senators from the seventeen smallest states represent less than eight percent of the national population, they constitute more than one-third of the total number of Senate seats, meaning they can block any Electoral College reform.

Third, any attempt to change the antiquated structure of the Senate—which some would say is downright undemocratic by giving a state like Wyoming, with less than 600,000 residents, the same representation as a state like California, with nearly 40 million—faces an even greater barrier than any other change. The Constitution specifically says that "no State, without its Consent, shall be deprived of its equal Suffrage in the Senate." Thus, any attempt to change the two-Senators-per-state structure can be blocked by just a single state. Short of a revolution, we are destined to live with this Senate structure for a very long time.

And lastly, the members of Congress benefit from the status quo; what would cause them to want to change that? It is an unfortunate fact that despite our government's failings, fixing structural defects has little mass appeal. Voters cast their ballots more on personalities and partisan allegiance. Campaigns to change our government's structure rarely gain large followings.

Readers who would like to understand why the three amendments that have managed to change aspects of our government's structure are the exceptions that prove the rule, should read the Appendix where I describe the unique circumstances that allowed each of those amendments to succeed. Given how rarely in our nation's history those circumstances have existed, I believe it would be unwise to focus on constitutional reform to fix the problems in our democracy. Instead, in the pages that follow, I present twelve individual acts of courage that can more quickly and effectively move us down that path.

PART I

★★★

CONGRESS

1

ACROSS THE GREAT DIVIDE

A SIMPLE ACT OF LEARNING: For members of Congress, from across the aisle and from distant parts of America, to tour each other's districts or states together, so they can better understand each other and our nation.

At the end of the day, most Americans don't care about Democratic ideas versus Republican ideas. We care about good ideas, regardless of their source. Most Americans just want Congress to work together to solve our nation's problems. But the seeds of congressional cooperation will not grow in barren soil; bipartisanship must be nurtured and fed. Congressional cooperation rests upon two basic ingredients: the first is to get to know members of the other party as real people, not just partisan opponents, and the second is to cultivate a sense of working for all Americans, not just those in a member's own district or state. Those two traits, as simple as they may be, are the necessary foundation for a Congress that produces results. And the good news is that those traits can be cultivated, but not in the bitterly partisan environment of Washington.

So not only do members of Congress need to leave the "echo chamber" of Washington more often, they also need to spend more time outside their own districts or states. They need to learn about the lives of all Americans, not just those back home. Americans worry about the country being on the wrong track, not just our own narrow slice of it. We understand that the well-being of our communities depends on the well-being of the nation as a whole. But do all the members of Congress understand that? Those who make the effort to broaden their knowledge of this vast country and its diverse people will be the ones best able to solve its problems.

And what better way to learn about America than jointly touring it with a counterpart from across the aisle? What better way for members of Congress to get to know one another—as real people from real places with shared American values—than to meet on each other's home turf? Spending time in each other's living rooms, backyards, and neighborhoods is the best way to build the personal relationships necessary to withstand, and eventually transform, the divisive nature of Washington.

So let us call upon the members of Congress to immerse themselves in the melting pot of America and to do so hand in hand with their supposed "opponents" across the aisle. They need not renounce their partisan ideals. Nor do they need to agree to like each other, although they may find—to their surprise—that they do. They simply need to meet on each other's turf, as fellow Americans, to begin understanding each other and America's diverse challenges and opportunities.

PARTISANS ARE PEOPLE TOO

The cause of the gridlock in Washington is not partisanship; it is partisanship run amok. We don't need to reach some "post-partisan promised land." In fact, trying to do so is a pipe dream. Political parties are an inevitable result of human nature: our proclivity to congregate with like-minded people. We find safety and strength in numbers. While the founding fathers idealistically imagined an America without political parties—indeed they built the Constitution around that very premise—no sooner had the ink on the Constitution dried than political factions began battling over whether it should be ratified. By the end of George Washington's first term as president, the founding fathers themselves had split into two opposing parties, the Federalists and the Democratic-Republicans, the very thing they hoped would never come to pass.

But two centuries later, we can see that political parties are not just "necessary evils." They are, in fact, essential elements of a functioning democracy. Political parties organize the citizenry's ideals into coherent sets of common values. They create order out of chaos, enabling the negotiation and compromise needed for a functioning government. Imagine the 435 voting members of the House of Representatives and the 100 members of the Senate trying to reach agreement without the organizing structure that political parties provide. Such a scenario would make today's Congress, in comparison, look like a well-oiled machine.

So what America needs is not less partisanship, but a new approach to partisanship. We need our leaders to get to know one other as real people, not partisan caricatures. We need our leaders to learn about America as a whole. Because ironically, in today's hyper-connected, web-linked, and social media networked world, our leaders are more disconnected from each other—and from everyday American life—than ever before.

PROVINCIALISM, PERPETUAL MOTION & PERSONAL ANIMOSITY

Despite the mobility afforded by modern American society, our leaders are surprisingly provincial. Indeed, rather than hiding their provincialism, they are proud of it. Politicians often tout how they were born in their district or state, graduated from the local high school, married their childhood sweetheart, and built a career in the community. Candidates use phrases like "lifelong resident," "fifth-generation," and "born and raised" as badges of honor. A sampling from current and recent congressional members' websites, both Democrat and Republican, rural and urban, is telling:

> "[Rep. Charles Rangel] has resided in a total of two places the whole of his life—the 132nd Street Harlem home in which he was born and raised, and his current apartment down the street on Lenox Avenue."

> "[Rep. Denny Rehberg] brings both the work ethic of a fifth-generation family rancher...and the core Montana values of integrity and personal accountability to the job with him every day..."

> "... A lifelong resident of the First District, [Rep. Earl L. "Buddy" Carter] was born and raised in Port Wentworth, Georgia...[and] married his college sweetheart."

> "A native of rural Bolton, Mississippi, [Rep. Bennie Thompson] has always been aware of the realities that plague the South. Viewing the experiences his family endured first hand became the catalyst for his passion for those who were oftentimes underserved...He married his college sweetheart, London Johnson of Mound Bayou, Mississippi in 1968, they remain happily married to this day."

Let me be clear: being rooted in the traditions of one's community is not a failing. It is something to celebrate. The problem, rather, is that too few members of Congress share their deep understanding of the hopes and dreams of their communities *with each other*. As a result, they come to see their supposed opponents across the aisle as caricatures rather than real human beings and fellow Americans.

It is fair to point out that provincialism in politics is nothing new. In the earliest years of the republic, a congressional member's journey to take their seat in Washington might have been their first foray outside their home state or even their home county.

But while politicians in that time were less exposed to the "outside world" than today, they were more exposed to *each other* than today. Once they arrived in Washington for the congressional session, they stayed. They may have been political opponents, but they were also neighbors. Lawmakers and government officials generally lodged within a stone's throw of Capitol Hill. The capitol was a place of intense social activity. Trapped together for weeks and months at a time, the nation's leaders mingled at parties, dinners and drinking establishments. Yes, they argued and fought, but they also formed the kinds of working relationships and friendships that can only come from long stretches of time spent in close quarters. Even through the end of World War II, Washington was a fairly compact city. Only in the post-war era—the golden age of the automobile—did our elected leaders spread out within the rapidly expanding Washington metropolis and begin to lose the sense of community so essential to the healthy functioning of our government.

But while the automobile may have struck the first blow against congressional collegiality, it was the modern jetliner more than anything else, that enabled members of Congress to succumb to the allure of nearly non-stop campaigning for re-election. The advent of cheap commercial jet air service in the late 1950s provided vastly more reliable and rapid travel than the propeller planes of the day, and by the mid-1960s, members of Congress were in a state of perpetual motion, flitting back and forth between Washington and their home states and districts. Congressional rubbing of elbows over food and drink faded into the background, and contact amongst lawmakers became increasingly limited to bitter wrangling in the halls of Congress.

The final blow came in the 1990s, when Congress adopted a three-day workweek. Members of Congress were now spending the majority of their time back in their districts and states. Their families no longer came to live in Washington, and the socializing amongst families that was an important part of congressional congeniality disappeared.

And so we arrive at today's state of affairs: members of Congress "drop by" Washington just long enough to cast votes, get drawn into often overly partisan debates, and be set upon by lobbyists. It's almost understandable that they would be so eager to get back home. A sampling of congressional members' websites is telling:

> "I have always believed that unless we are called to Washington to vote, my time is best spent in our district and I come home every weekend. (Representative Gene Green, D-Houston)"

> "I work in Washington, but I live in Texas. It is vitally important to the representation of my district that I am here as much as possible meeting and speaking with the

people in the 2nd District. (Representative Ted Poe, R-Texas)"

"[Denny] favors Montana-grown solutions, which is why as Montana's Congressman he has maintained that pledge to this day by traveling to all 56 counties each congressional term. (Representative Denny Rehberg, R-Montana)"

"When Mike is not working in the nation's capital or visiting the 150 towns in the Fourth Congressional District, he spends time with his family and enjoys hunting and fishing right here in Arkansas. (Representative Mike Ross, R-Arkansas)"

"In 1998, Chuck was elected to the U.S. Senate...Chuck kicked off his first Senate term by announcing he would visit each of New York's 62 counties every year, a tradition he continues today. Doing so has enabled Chuck to keep in touch with voters from every corner of the state. (Senator Charles Schumer, D-New York)"

Perhaps their intentions are good—a desire to stay in close contact with their constituents. Cynics, on the other hand, will say that it's all about campaigning. But whichever is true (and maybe it's both), the fact is that the current approaches to serving in Congress aren't working; we need members of Congress to try something different. If the Washington environment is not conducive to working together—and everything seems to indicate that it isn't—then members of Congress should find someplace else to do it. Because in addition to the provincialism that narrows our lawmakers' views, and the perpetual motion that has them continually fleeing back to their home states, the last part of the problem is the personal animosity and polarization rampant in politics today. And for that we can thank the rise of television, the internet, and even the smart phone.

December 7, 1941—the day that Pearl Harbor was attacked—may have been, as Franklin Roosevelt said, a "day that will forever live in infamy," but an event five months earlier may have caused far more lasting damage to American democracy. On July 1, 1941, the first commercial television broadcast was aired in the U.S., a ticking political time bomb whose destructive effects on American politics would be realized only years later.

With the nation's focused attention to the war effort, television was slow to take hold. At the close of World War II, only one in a thousand American households—a total of 44,000 nationwide—owned a television set. But with the return of millions of soldiers from overseas, the sudden availability of America's massive wartime manufacturing capacity for peacetime purposes, and the aching desire of a nation weary of war to enjoy more "creature comforts," the television industry blossomed.

By 1954, half of all American families—over 25 million—owned one of the new devices. And on April 22, 1954—during the height of the Cold War and its anti-Communist hysteria—the political time bomb exploded when the first witness at the now-infamous "McCarthy hearings" stepped in front of the cameras. The first-ever nationally-televised congressional inquiry captured the nation's attention for nearly two months. The media circus had come to town and American politics would never be the same again.

It took little time for politicians to realize that in this new era, style mattered more than substance. Whether they liked it or not, reasoned discourse failed to capture the public's attention as much as partisan bombast. It wasn't long before politicians no longer looked each other in the eye when they spoke. They stared into the camera's lens as statesmanship gave way to showmanship.

The advent of the 24-hour news channel and the internet brought the state of American politics to a new low, and with today's proliferation of mobile devices—with their built-in cameras and video recorders—things have deteriorated even further. Because nothing is private anymore, politicians need to watch every word they say, lest they be recorded deviating, even slightly, from the rigid party line. The end result is that members of the opposing parties rarely meet face to face to speak candidly about addressing the nation's challenges. Charles Peters, in *Washington Monthly* (April/May 2010), wrote:

> The empty tables of the senators' private dining room have become a symbol of the bitter partisanship that divides American politics. 'Nobody goes there anymore,' [Senator] Max Baucus recently remarked. 'When I was here ten, fifteen, thirty, years ago that was the place you would go to talk to [other] senators, let your hair down, just kind of compare notes, no spouses allowed, no staff, nobody.'

An interesting perspective is provided by Congressman Rick Nolan of Minnesota, who served in the House of Representatives in the 1970s, and returned in 2013 after a 32-year absence (his aides jokingly refer to him as "Rick van Winkle"). Matt Viser wrote in the *Boston Globe* about Congressman Nolan:

> Back then, in the 1970s, Nolan brought his wife and four young children from Minnesota to live with him in Washington. He and his family even spent weekends with

congressional colleagues camping, hiking, and attending bipartisan barbecues...[now] he no longer recognizes the world he has found himself in. Washington has become an increasingly dysfunctional place. There may be no better way to see the shift than through the eyes of Nolan. He sees a Congress that does not meet as often, where few members linger on Capitol Hill. Lawmakers jet in and out of the city's airport on a dizzying weekly schedule. Representatives pass in hallways but do not know each other's names...'It's quite dramatically, profoundly different,' Nolan says. 'In big ways and small ways.' Emblematic is a small change that has become one of Nolan's pet peeves: The House dining room, where he fondly remembers sitting at all hours of the day with his congressional colleagues, now closes in the early afternoon. Lost is an opportunity to make the personal connections that today's Congress so sorely lacks.

So how can we bring back congressional camaraderie, or at least a modicum of respect? We can't turn the clock back on technology. We're not going to get rid of air travel, television or the internet, and we can't stop our politicians from using them. But the very fact that our leaders can so easily flee Washington every weekend makes it easy to bring someone from the other party back home with them. Consider Democratic Senator Schumer from New York, or former Republican Congressman Rehberg from Montana, as examples, with their habits of visiting every one of their state's counties each year. What could be easier than to bring a fellow member of Congress, from across the aisle, along on some of those visits?

LEADING THE WAY

Some politicians have started down this path. Take Republican Representative Dan Benishek, who represents a rural district in northern Michigan, and former Representative Hansen Clarke, a Democrat who has spent most of his life in his urban Detroit district. As different as they may be (at least on the surface), they hit it off when they met during the 2011 congressional freshman orientation. That fall, they teamed up for tours of each other's districts.

Mr. Benishek was quoted as saying: "I'm not the type of the person who doesn't want to talk to people on the other side of the aisle or screams vilifying statements at people, and neither is he. You don't do any good by calling people names." Mr. Clarke described the tours in this manner: "We are one state and one economy. Rep. Benishek and I can reach across the aisle and work together to bring jobs to Michigan."

First, the two Congressmen spent a day touring Detroit. Benishek, who sits on the Committee on Veterans Affairs, found it eye-opening to learn about homeless veterans needing to use a Veterans Affairs (VA) clinic just to be able to take a shower. As a result of the visit, he says, the two politicians and the Veterans Affairs Committee began working to improve the VA's support of homeless veterans. Likewise, when Clarke, who sits on the Homeland Security Committee, visited Benishek's district in the Upper Peninsula, the two were able to talk about border security challenges that the committee was grappling with. And of course, throughout their time together, the two looked at the issue of jobs in Michigan and how to work together to increase them.

That same year, in Colorado, two members of the state's congressional delegation conducted a similar joint tour. Despite political differences on many issues, Republican Congressman

Cory Gardner and Democratic Senator Michael Bennet joined together for the common purpose of job creation, conducting a joint tour of businesses in Gardner's northern Colorado district. Said Senator Bennet: "Anything we can do to work together across the aisle is important for the people of our state." Representative Gardner weighed in by saying: "This isn't a Republican or Democrat issue. Getting our constituents back to work is something we both have to focus on."

These types of bipartisan tours are not just good for the country; they can pay off for politicians. Consider what the website *ColoradoPeakPolitics.com* said about Gardner and Bennet's tour: "Trips like this are great press for a first term Congressman…[and] show that Gardner is such an effective and likable legislator that members of the opposing party, even inside the [Colorado] delegation, want to work with him."

These examples demonstrate the good that can come when politicians are courageous enough to cross the aisle and engage as real people. So shouldn't we expect the same from more members of Congress? Shouldn't we ask them to meet on each other's turf, to break bread together, to meet each other's families and constituents? Whether New Yorker or New Mexican, Alaskan or Arkansan, our leaders are all Americans; they will gain favor by acting that way.

Imagine a Republican Representative from rural Louisiana touring an urban Los Angeles district with his or her Democratic counterpart. Picture the two of them meeting with urban constituents, attending neighborhood meetings, learning firsthand about gang violence and urban decay, traveling on public transportation, and touring the region's thriving entertainment industry. Then imagine them traveling together to Louisiana, to learn firsthand about hurricane damage, Mississippi River flooding, the Gulf of Mexico oil fields, fishing, and farming.

Or picture a Democratic Senator from Massachusetts spending a week in Wyoming with his or her Republican counterpart, hearing from citizens about western issues, such as energy development, water rights, ranching, and mining. Then imagine them traveling to Massachusetts to tour that region's institutions of higher education, its tourism industry, its manufacturing centers, and its vibrant high-tech industries.

Think about your own Senators or Representative. Wouldn't you like to see them bringing home colleagues from the other party and other parts of the country, to show them the needs of your district or state? Isn't that in your best interest, as well as the best interest of the nation?

These joint tours would go beyond just building relationships. They could shift the attitude of Americans toward government itself. Think about the message of national unity that would be conveyed when the bipartisan tour comes to town. Residents, business owners, and local officials would turn out to meet these representatives from other parts of the country. Positive local press coverage would be generated. The electorate would see these tours as courageous and patriotic acts.

Let's not forget that, in addition to salaries of nearly $200,000 per year, members of Congress are reimbursed for most, if not all, of their travel back home, no matter how frequent. So it's quite reasonable to call upon them to use some of that travel money to unite, rather than divide, the nation. Members of Congress eagerly travel to far-flung corners of the globe for the stated reason of understanding foreign policy issues, but rarely travel to another part of the U.S. with to learn about American issues. Rarer still do they do it one-on-one with a member of the other party. Imagine if every congressional member going overseas on congressional business matched that travel with a bipartisan tour here at home. If he or she were to spend a week in Paris on foreign policy affairs, then they could also spend a week with one of their so-called opponents touring each other's backyards.

Joint tours would be a simple and straightforward way for our leaders to get to know each other as real human beings, as fellow Americans, as compatriots in the mission to build a safe and prosperous America. The relationships that would result—perhaps even friendships—could transform the tone of Washington politics and create a foundation for the bipartisan problem-solving America so desperately needs.

2

THE RED BADGE OF COURAGE
Walking the talk

A CONGRESSIONAL PLEDGE OF HONOR: "If I vote for war I will go to war, joining our troops on the field of battle."

★ ★ ★

Few acts of Congress carry weightier consequences than taking the nation to war, yet few acts are so far removed from the typical member of Congress's comprehension. No more than one out of every five members of the current Congress has served in the military and few of them have ever been on the front lines. It is time we ask our leaders to show the same courage that our military servicemen and women show day in and day out. It is time they experience first-hand the consequences of their decisions. If we, as a nation, are to go to war, shouldn't our leaders be standing alongside the troops?

This pledge of honor is not a call for members of Congress to take up full-time military service, but rather to undertake special tours of duty, up to several weeks in length, during congressional recess. War would no longer be just an abstract notion within a policy debate; it would be made real for Congress, just as it is for those who do the fighting. When the members of Congress start putting their own safety on the line, their decisions will be based on more than just political motives. They will, for once, have some "skin in the game."

How can we expect our leaders to make wise decisions about going to war if they don't have an understanding of it? Representative Tulsi Gabbard (D-HI), an Iraq war veteran, was quoted in a *New York Times* article (February 17, 2015) as saying that she wondered whether "the leaders of our country and those in positions of making these decisions really understand what the impacts of their decisions were…One of the reasons I ran for Congress was to make sure we didn't repeat the mistakes of the past, of going into war without a clear strategy."

Let me be clear: this is neither an anti-war nor a pro-war issue. It is a call for our leaders to "walk the talk." It is a call to bring a renewed sense of heroism, honor, and shared sacrifice to Congress.

EDUCATING CONGRESS

> [He tried to] prove to himself that he would not run from a battle. Previously, he had never felt obliged to wrestle too seriously with this question…But here he was confronted with a thing of moment. It had suddenly appeared to him that perhaps in a battle he might run. He was forced to admit that as far as war was concerned he knew nothing of himself.
>
> — *Stephen Crane, The Red Badge of Courage*

The time was when every American schoolchild read *The Red Badge of Courage*, the classic Civil War novel following 18-year-old Henry Fleming's journey as a Union soldier. Doubt, cowardice and shame dog the young soldier and in his first taste of combat he turns and runs. But eventually his experiences on the field of battle bring about a change, a maturing, a sense of greater purpose. By the novel's end, he emerges a hero. Moved to save his fellow soldiers, he displays courage unknown even to himself. Unarmed, he carries the flag into battle, earning his redemption.

More than 150 years later, America's brave soldiers continue to put their lives on the line, far from view and far too little noticed. From the halls of Congress to our own living rooms, we have become complacent about the dangers our soldiers face in distant corners of the globe. At the same time, our leaders are shocked when one of them is threatened with violence here at home. Not long ago, our nation witnessed the tragic shooting of Representative Gabrielle Giffords, a young Congresswoman from Arizona. Representative Giffords survived, but six other victims lost their lives. Rep. Raul Grijalva (D-AZ), was quoted as saying: "We all enter this life of public service and being elected officials. We don't enter it believing that it's a life and death situation."

Mr. Grijalva may have been voicing a sentiment shared by many in elected office: that while public service may entail hardships, the risk of physical harm is not one of them. Yet every enlistee entering military service does just what Mr. Grijalva rejects for himself—entering into a life or death situation. Surely it's not asking too much of our leaders—who hold the power to place our brave soldiers in harm's way—to stand alongside them, if even for just a short while.

A friend of mine—a college teacher—related to me how one of her students, returning from combat in Iraq, was struggling with re-entry into civilian life. "The thing is" the student said, "that no one here knows what it's like to be willing to take a bullet for your fellow soldiers." How true. So few of us, here at home, truly understand the selflessness of America's soldiers.

And what of our leaders? In what ways are they willing to "take a bullet" for America? What would that look like, in the halls of Congress? Would it be a vote for a bill that moves America forward, but that comes at political cost? Speaking up for constituencies whose voices are silenced? Crossing the aisle to engage with one's so-called "opponents"? A member of Congress who's faced danger on the battlefield—who's known fear and risen above it—is the type of man or woman who will have the courage, here at home, to take a bullet for America.

What's more, by asking members of Congress to stand alongside our troops, we are not just asking them to do the right thing for our country, we are offering them a precious gift: the opportunity to discover a courage they may not have known lay within. And they will return that gift to us, carrying their newfound sense of bravery back to the halls of Congress. Courage awakened in the face of danger does not fall easily back asleep.

The Vanishing Veteran

In the current Congress, roughly one in five members has served in the military. Just twenty years ago at least half had served, and thirty years ago, three out of every four members of Congress were veterans. So, in just three decades, Congress's military makeup has been entirely turned upside down: in 1980 most congressional members were veterans, today most have no military experience at all. Possibly no other aspect of the makeup of Congress has ever changed so dramatically in such a short period—not race, nor religion, nor gender.

The number of veterans in Congress only keeps decreasing, even with an influx of new members who served in Iraq and Afghanistan. The 101 veterans in the current 114th Congress is 7 fewer than in the 113th Congress (108 veterans) and 17 fewer than in the 112th Congress (118 members).

What's more, amongst the veterans in Congress today, few have experienced combat. No more than four Senators, out of the one hundred in office, claim to be combat veterans (and two of those Senators' claims are disputed). In the House of Representatives, barely a third of the 81 members with military service are combat veterans. So, among the 535 voting members of Congress, few have directly experienced the nature of war.

The same trend can be seen in the U.S. presidency. In the 2012 presidential race, for the first time in nearly seven decades, neither major-party candidate had performed military service. The two major-party presidential candidates in the current 2016 continue that trend. What does it mean for our country to have a Congress making decisions about war, when the vast majority of its members have no direct experience of it, and a president, as Commander-in-Chief, with a similar lack of understanding of the realities of the waging of war?

The decreasing number of veterans in Washington mirrors the trend in the overall population. The percentage of Americans performing military service has steadily declined since the draft was eliminated in 1973. At the height of World War II, nearly one in ten Americans was on active duty, whereas in the decade of warfare in Iraq and Afghanistan following the 9/11 attacks, that number was one in two hundred. From 2000 to 2010 the number of U.S. veterans dropped from approximately 26 million to less than 23 million and is expected to decrease to less than 16 million by 2035.

In recent years, some have called for a reinstatement of the draft, not only to ensure sufficient enlistment, but also to sharpen the focus of our elected leaders when making decisions about going to war. In 2006, Rep. Charlie Rangel (D-NY) said "There's no question in my mind that this president and this administration would never have invaded Iraq, especially on the flimsy evidence that was presented to the Congress, if indeed we had a draft and members of Congress and the administration thought that their kids from their communities would be placed in harm's way."

Veterans groups have long sought to place more of their own in office as a means of creating a Congress more in touch with the realities of war. That has proved to be a tough battle. Incumbency plays a much stronger role in winning election than veteran status. In the 2014 elections, more than 80% of veterans running against incumbents lost. So if we want our leaders to be able to make better-informed decisions about war, then instead of seeking to elect more veterans, we must make veterans out of the leaders we elect.

How It Would Work

Members of Congress would not just drop everything and march off to the battlefield. We need them to perform their legislative duties. That's why we elected them to office. There is ample time, however, for them to fulfill their legislative responsibilities and also perform a "congressional tour of duty." Over the course of a year Congress is typically out of session for anywhere from four to six months. If congressional military service were to involve a week of training "in-country" and then three weeks on the battlefield, that represents only one month out of the generous recess time Congress enjoys.

The military roles that members of Congress would perform would need to be carefully selected. Lawmakers do not have the time to become as fully trained as regular troops. What's more, many are older than the typical soldier. But they can still play a variety of roles supporting the troops in the field of combat: medics, drivers, technicians, or simply observers. Almost any activity would suffice, as long as it is not a cushy job in a protected zone far from the front lines. These missions should be acts of courage, not comfort.

This pledge would apply to any vote in support of military action, not just a declaration of war. The last war declared by the U.S. Congress was World War II, but since then we have engaged in military conflicts in places like Korea, Vietnam, Panama, Grenada, Yugoslavia, Iraq, Afghanistan and Libya. In many of those cases, Congress played a decision-making role by passing resolutions in support of the military action or by authorizing funding.

Even a handful of members of Congress taking this pledge could transform the whole Congress. Imagine the moral high ground they would occupy. If just one out of every 10 members of Congress—44 Representatives and 10 Senators—were to take this pledge, those 54 men and women would set a standard of honor and accountability for the other 481 members of Congress to look up to.

HONOR, COURAGE AND INTEGRITY

I acknowledge that this proposed act of courage raises important questions. Its consequences are greater than many of the other acts in this book. Would this act place an excessive burden on the troops? No more so, I would argue, than the well-accepted practice of embedding reporters with the troops. At the beginning of the Iraq War in 2003, an estimated 570 to 750 reporters were in such roles.

It might also be argued that a member of Congress in a combat zone would be an attractive target, thereby increasing the danger to the troops. That concern could be minimized by requiring congressional military service to be done discretely. It need only be announced after it is completed.

The fact is that the conduct of war by a free democratic nation always involves trade-offs. For example, the First Amendment guarantee of a free press and the attendant reporting on U.S. military operations could be argued to increase the risk, at times, to our troops. But we accept that possible increased risk because a free press is so central to American values. Similarly, military codes of ethics balance the goal of military victory against America's commitment to basic human rights.

In the same way, the burden and risks of this proposed pledge of congressional honor must be weighed against the benefits of national unity and of having elected leaders who understand the decisions they are making. The nation will gain much value from leaders with a personal—not just political—stake in those decisions. I believe that the men and women of our military would not resent any additional burden or risk, but rather, would feel honored by the presence of public servants with the courage to be by their side.

In the years since the tragic events of 9/11, our nation has been embroiled in harsh prolonged warfare overseas. Yet because so much of the fighting has been done by a small fraction of the American people—often outside of the public view—our nation has lacked a true sense of shared sacrifice. This pledge by members of Congress to stand alongside our brave soldiers could be a step toward building that sense of national unity.

What's more, in today's world, military success increasingly depends on winning the hearts and minds of foreign populations. This pledge's demonstration of honor and sacrifice at the highest levels of our government would provide our military with a tool that few other countries possess. Let us not underestimate the respect that America would gain when our leaders show themselves to be men and women of courage, honor, and integrity. That's the American way. That can be the American future.

3

FIRST, WALK A MILE
Walking in the shoes of ordinary Americans

A SIMPLE ACT OF UNDERSTANDING: For members of Congress to climb down from Congress's ivory towers and "go undercover" to learn how the rest of America lives.

M embers of Congress are entrusted with decisions that impact greatly on everyday American life, but how well do they understand the daily lives of most Americans? One out of every two members of Congress is a millionaire, in stark contrast to the one out of one hundred Americans in that elite class.

This is not an indictment of our elected leaders for their wealth, nor a charge that such riches *inherently* prevent an understanding of the day-to-day struggles of average Americans—indeed, some of America's most revered leaders have been among our wealthiest citizens. But most politicians, no matter how smart, principled, or patriotic they may be, face an uphill battle to govern effectively and wisely when their wealth puts them so out of touch with the lives of ordinary Americans.

So let us call upon the members of Congress to climb down from their ivory towers and "go undercover" to learn the facts of life of today's America. Not in the style of old-school fact-finding missions, done as grand public affairs, with reporters and local officials in tow. Instead, these should be missions to live and breathe the lives of ordinary Americans, done as quietly and incognito as possible. This could mean taking up residence in a poverty-stricken neighborhood of Washington, D.C; seeking health care at a local emergency room; spending a weekend in a federal prison; or working in a variety of low-wage or middle-class jobs. There is no end to the ways our wealthy leaders can learn about 21st century American life.

Only in this manner can members of Congress truly understand the ways that their actions—or failures to act—directly affect Americans' lives. If we are to have government of the people, by the people, and for the people, then our leaders need to learn how the American people live.

THE CREATURE COMFORTS OF CONGRESSIONAL LIFE

The disparity in wealth between those in the top tier of the American population and those below has captured America's attention in the wake of the "Great Recession." Less talked about, but perhaps even more important, is the divide between our elected leaders in Washington and the rest of us.

The average American household earns roughly $54,000 per year. After paying for food, clothing, housing, health insurance, taxes, retirement contributions, possibly some savings for the kids' college tuition, perhaps a modest vacation, the average American household has little, if any, money left over at the end of the year. Often all that the average family has accumulated is debt. Even more troubling is the fact that the average household income of minorities is far lower, at $40,000 per year for Hispanic households and $36,000 per year for black households.

Clearly, life for an increasing number of Americans is lived paycheck to paycheck, and even managing that is an accomplishment.

On the other hand, recent figures show that the average net worth of a U.S. Senator is more than $10 million and the average net worth of a member of a U.S. Representative is more than $7 million. And those numbers just keep increasing. The median net worth of Congress's members increased by 15 percent from 2004 to 2010, even as that of the average American dropped by 8 percent.

Few members of Congress could be called poor or even middle-class. How could they? Even when poor or middle-class candidates manage to win office, their congressional salaries instantly place them among the ranks of America's upper-class. Members of the House and Senate are paid $174,000 per year, with higher pay for the Majority and Minority Leaders ($193,400) and Speaker of the House ($223,500). Add the generous congressional benefits and their spouses' earnings, and the result is that member of Congress live sheltered lives with few of the financial worries of the average American.

Let me say it again: I'm not indicting politicians for their financial success. Most Americans admire those who have succeeded at the America dream. Most of us aspire to a greater degree of comfort and security and a greater ability to give back to our communities. Who would turn down the benefits that a congressional member's wealth affords—new cars, a more comfortable house, nicer vacations, eating out more often? Few Americans would choose to use the emergency room for primary care if instead they could afford a good doctor. Few would choose food stamps if they had other means to feed their families.

And let's be fair: not all members of Congress are in the ranks of the super-rich, living in isolated gated estates. Some, while far better off than most of us, are deeply embedded in our communities and are our friends and neighbors. But they still face vastly different day-to-day realities. They are not choosing between car repairs and groceries; they are not worried about affording college tuition for their children; they are not worried that a major medical incident could wipe out whatever meager savings they have. An estimated 5 million Americans lost their homes to foreclosure as a result of the recent Great Recession. Were any members of Congress among those 5 million? It is doubtful.

The issue is not whether members of Congress deserve such comfort. The issue is simply whether their ability to be effective lawmakers—to do what is best for the average American—may be hampered by the possibility that they have forgotten, and maybe never knew, what it's like to *be* an average American.

You Can't Solve A Problem That You Don't Understand

> Tell me and I'll forget; show me and I may remember; involve me and I'll understand.
> —*Chinese Proverb*

Good decision-making depends on good understanding, and for good understanding there is no substitute for direct experience. Hearings, briefings, and reports—the typical ways that members of Congress learn about the issues—lack the richness of on-the-ground experience. And I'm not talking about the types of staged experiences that members of Congress have on those occasions when they leave their congressional hearing rooms. It's one thing to be shown the hospital emergency room by the head of the hospital and a well-coached staff; it's quite another to show up in the middle of the night, with no health insurance, seeking help for a sick child.

The value of learning the underlying realities about the issues was reflected in a statement by Speaker of the House Paul Ryan, quoted in the June 20, 2016 edition of the *New Yorker*: "There was a time that I would talk about a difference between 'makers' and 'takers' in our country, referring to people who accepted government benefits...But, as I spent more time listening, and really learning the root causes of poverty, I realized something. I realized that I was wrong."

Some politicians have already demonstrated a willingness to "get their hands dirty." In Maine, during the 2008 election season, Republican 1st Congressional District candidate Charlie Summers embarked on a "30 Jobs in 30 Days" campaign. Over the course of a month he did everything from working at a sandwich shop to delivering fuel oil to washing hair at a beauty salon to cleaning tanks at a brew pub. Summers, an Iraq War veteran, explained his campaign: "It's about meeting people in their everyday environment and listening to their concerns, not only to learn how they earn a living, but to learn how they feel about the economy."

In another example, a small handful of members of Congress have stepped forward in recent years to take the "Food Stamp Challenge," developed by the group *Fighting Poverty with Faith*. The Food Stamp Challenge requires participants to live on a food stamp budget, most recently set at $31.50 per week in 2011. "I just wanted to get a real-world sense of what it means to survive on the average food stamp allocation, just to get a sense of what people go through," said Representative Chris Van Hollen (D-MD). Representative James McGovern (D-MA), who participated in the challenge in 2007, said that he and his wife had "gained valuable insights from [their] experience on a very tight budget."

Freshman Representative Joe Walsh (R-IL) stood by his 2010 campaign pledge to forego federal health insurance, despite the obstacles that his wife's pre-existing condition would present in finding private insurance. "[We] are going to have to go through the struggles that a lot of Americans go through," said Walsh, "trying to find insurance in the individual market and having to deal with problems of preexisting conditions."

One member of Congress has gone so far as to make undercover missions his trademark. Representative Mike Quigley (D-IL) bills himself as the "Undercover Congressman." In recent years, he has worked alongside his constituents in dozens of jobs, from delivering mail to making candies at the Mars factory, busing restaurant tables, and working on a city garbage truck. In doing so, he says, he has learned far more than he could within the DC beltway or from constituent letters.

MISSION: POSSIBLE

So what America needs is a squad of "Undercover Congressmen and Congresswomen" taking on (relatively) secret missions to understand the lives of ordinary Americans. These missions could be short-term investigations to understand particular aspects of a policy issue or longer-term immersions in the lives of average Americans. Here are some possibilities:

Urban poverty: Over 45 million Americans were living in poverty in 2014, representing over 14% of the U.S. population, according to the U.S. Census Bureau. Poverty rates are highest in America's cities, where over 20% of the population is at or below the poverty line. Opportunities abound, even within commuting distance of the capitol, for members of Congress to do a "residency" in an area of urban poverty. Within a one-hour drive of Capitol Hill can be found some of the poorest urban neighborhoods in the country; in Washington,

Baltimore, and other nearby urban enclaves. A member of Congress from a rural part of the country or from an elite urban background could take up residence in one of these neighborhoods—alone or as a guest of a local family—to gain a better understanding of how federal policies impact urban poverty.

Business: Why not go undercover with a startup company to learn the impacts of government regulations and how government programs could better support business growth? Or a member of Congress from an urban area could immerse him or herself in a fishing or farming community facing the pressures of government regulations and global competition. As members of Congress grapple with issues of international trade, government regulation, and job creation, they would benefit greatly by understanding the on-the-ground realities of businesspeople in America.

Senior issues: Few, if any, members of Congress—even those beyond the typical retirement age—face the same challenges as most senior citizens: living on limited incomes, balancing food and medical expenses, and navigating mazes of red tape to obtain benefits. Surely there are senior citizens who would welcome congressional members into their homes, in order to show them the day-to-day challenges of aging in America. Or why not a stay with a working family caring for aging parents? This would provide an understanding of the struggles such families face balancing the demands of working, caring for their elderly loved ones, raising their children, and other day-to-day activities.

The Environment: Most members of Congress have no idea what it's like to live next to a landfill, an incinerator, an oil refinery, or a chemical plant. Or to manage, or work in, one of those facilities. Let them undertake missions to experience how those facilities impact the lives of workers and nearby residents, in both positive and negative ways. Let them spend time alongside the owners or managers of such facilities to understand the challenges they face in meeting government regulations, ensuring the financial soundness of their operations, and being good "industrial neighbors" in their communities.

Many members of Congress also have no direct experience with the daily lives of Americans who make their living from our natural resources—farmers, loggers, ranchers, miners, fishermen and women. Undercover missions spent working alongside these Americans would give an understanding of the difficult balances that must be struck between producing needed products and ensuring a healthy environment.

The Criminal Justice System: It is widely reported that the U.S. puts more of its citizens behind bars than any other country in the world. On average, we have nearly five times as many prisoners—in proportion to our population—as other western industrialized countries. But the effect that this high rate of incarceration has on crime is uncertain. On the one hand, we are harsher on nonviolent criminals than countries like England, Australia, and Canada and we have lower rates of nonviolent crime than those countries. On the other hand, despite also being harsher on *violent* criminals than such countries, we have much higher rates of violent crime than they.

Members of Congress could explore a variety of aspects of the criminal justice system: accompanying police officers as they make their rounds; shadowing district attorneys through their day-to-day duties; spending time in the offices of attorneys and judges to learn about the challenges they face. They could arrange to go undercover as defendants and even inmates to experience our nation's courts and correctional facilities from the perspective of those moving through them.

Healthcare: Undercover missions could include seeking primary care at a hospital emergency room or public health clinic; accompanying doctors and nurses on their rounds; meeting with hospital administrators, patients, and insurance company personnel to get their views about our healthcare system; attempting to settle an insurance claim; seeking insurance company approval for services; and shadowing nursing assistants and other lower-skilled workers who provide front-line personal care to patients.

Immigration: Imagine what members of Congress could learn by going undercover with families in America's southern border regions, or with immigrants residing in the U.S., both legal and illegal. Or they could spend time on the job with employers who use immigrant labor, or accompany border patrol agents on their day-to-day activities. More courageous undercover missions could involve simulating illegal entry into the U.S., such as getting to the border, crossing over, and then traveling through the U.S.

It would be particularly useful for congressional members to undertake missions based on their committee assignments. The

Senate has 20 standing committees and the House has 21; in addition, there are four standing joint committees. The "real work" of the Congress takes place in these committees and subcommittees, each of which focuses on a particular area of policy. Committees are where bills are drafted and where the decisions are made whether to send them to the full Congress for passage. But members of Congress are often assigned to committees for political reasons, not because of any particular knowledge of the committee's area of work. That makes undercover missions based on committee assignments all the more necessary. Lawmakers could also consider doing missions in bipartisan pairs; this would help them understand each other's differing perspectives on the issues they are investigating, which could lead to finding bipartisan solutions.

Would these missions add time to the busy schedules of lawmakers? Yes. Would it be time well-spent? Absolutely. Our lawmakers need to understand the important issues they are voting on and learn first-hand the ways their decisions impact the American people.

4

LEADERSHIP IS A TEAM SPORT: ASKING FOR HELP

A SIMPLE ACT OF TEAMWORK: For members of Congress to form advisory committees of the "best and brightest" of their constituents—from across the political spectrum—to help craft solutions to America's problems.

The 21st century world is one of interconnections, networks, and collaboration. But do members of Congress do enough to tap into the wisdom and creativity of their constituents? America doesn't need politicians who think they have all the answers—that's not even possible. We need politicians who can bring people together to *create solutions.* A "go it alone" attitude might have worked in earlier times, but it's not the type of leadership we need for the challenges of today. It's not how our nation will solve its problems.

Authors Warren Bennis and Patricia Ward Biederman talk about team-based leadership in their 1998 book *Organizing Genius: The Secrets of Creative Collaboration:* "Whether it is midnight rider Paul Revere or basketball's Michael Jordan in the 1990s, we are a nation enamored of heroes...In our society leadership is too often seen as an inherently individual phenomenon. And yet we all know that cooperation and collaboration grow more important every day...Throughout history, groups of people, often without conscious design, have successfully blended individual and collective effort to create something new and wonderful... In a society as complex and technologically sophisticated as ours, the most urgent projects require the coordinated contributions of many talented people." The authors highlight the astounding successes of six "Great Groups" ranging from the Manhattan Project to Apple Computer. Perhaps the most emblematic team effort they describe is Lockheed-Martin's famed "Skunk Works" which, over the past 70 years, has produced some of the world's most innovative aircraft. The term "skunk works" has come to epitomize the idea of a small highly autonomous group, using unconventional approaches to create "disruptive" products and solutions.

In today's world, taking a team approach to congressional service is more important than ever. The demands on congressional members are immense; the number of bills to review, the complexity of the issues, and the amount of information to absorb all keep getting greater. Even with the help of their advisors, they can't give sufficient attention to all of the nation's challenges.

A solution to this dilemma, however, exists: a member of Congress could enlist the help of his or her most talented constituents in a constituent advisory committee—the political equivalent of a skunk works. Its members—Democrats, Republicans and independents alike—would represent a range of community interests: business, the environment, low-income populations, healthcare, education, and more. Their charge would be to tackle the difficult issues facing Congress.

Would the committee have the final say? Of course not. But its advice would be invaluable. If it were to reach agreement on a solution to a particular national challenge, the member of Congress would have a powerful platform from which to advance the proposal. If its members were to *fail* to agree on a particular issue, its advice would still be valuable; the committee might report several options to consider, along with the reasons for their differences.

To succeed, a constituent committee needs to be properly run. Its meetings should be open to the public. Its members should include a range of political views and none should be current elected officials. The committee should be run by a neutral facilitator, trained to resolve conflicts and help the group solve problems. The committee should use on-line and in-person methods to involve the public.

Some members of Congress have at least partly ventured down this path. Several lawmakers have convened constituent advisory councils for veterans affairs, such as Rep. John Shimkus (R-IL), Rep. Tim Griffin (R-AR), Rep. Linda Sánchez (D-CA), Rep. Steve Pearce (R-NM), and Rep. Kathy Hochul (D-NY). Tackling different issues, Rep. Chris Gibson (R-NY) has created advisory groups to assist him with agriculture, energy and watershed issues.

Other members of Congress—from the most liberal to the most conservative—have created "youth advisory councils." At one end of the political spectrum is Representative Sam Johnson (R-TX), a decorated combat veteran of the Korean and Vietnam wars, and the most conservative member of Congress in 2011, according to the *National Journal.* At the other end is Jared Polis, a Democratic Representative from the liberal enclave of Boulder, Colorado, the first openly gay parent in Congress and a member of the Congressional Progressive Caucus. Yet despite their political differences, both men share a commitment to bringing young constituents into the political process.

Representative Johnson first convened his youth advisory council in 2004, "[to] provide Johnson greater perspective and insight on issues important to our younger generation." Similarly, Representative Polis's office runs two youth advisory councils, one in Denver and one in Fort Collins, that "meet throughout the year to discuss issues, organize educational events, and generally share what's on the minds of Colorado's young people." Each council is made up of high school students representing the geographic, cultural, and ideological diversity of Colorado's Second Congressional District.

Another team-based approach employed by several members of Congress is the use of bipartisan nominating committees for political appointments. California Senator Dianne Feinstein, for example, has established bipartisan advisory committees to screen and interview applicants for District Court Judges, U.S. Attorneys and U.S. Marshals. The committees then recommend nominees to the Senator. "I take seriously my responsibility to recommend nominees to the president and believe that a bipartisan, merit-based process is the best way to go," says Senator Feinstein. "These committees are made up of highly regarded attorneys who know their legal communities well. I am confident that the committee members will do their utmost to help me identify the most qualified candidates for the positions."

These are good first steps. But we need members of Congress to take the team approach to the next level. Today's challenges are interconnected. My research has failed to uncover a single member of Congress who has convened a standing bipartisan constituent committee to tackle the wide range of issues facing our nation.

Except, that is, for the handful of youth advisory committees. These youth advisory committees are important. In fact, every member of Congress would be well-advised to have one. There is even a campaign underway to establish a "Presidential Youth Council" to advise the president; a resolution in support of the idea introduced in the House of Representatives has been endorsed by over 50 members from both parties. But youth committees can only go so far. It's time for members of Congress to convene advisory groups of their *adult* constituents.

At the state level, at least one legislator—Representative Doris Kelley, of Cedar Falls, Iowa—has done this very thing. As the following letter to the *Cedar Falls Courier* shows, it can produce not only good policy, but good politics:

> Kudos [are] extended to Rep. Doris Kelley for establishing the first in the state legislative Constituent Advisory Committee. For the past four years, Rep. Kelley has asked one Republican, one Democrat, and one Independent per each of House District 20's wards and precincts to serve on the advisory board. She meets with the district's representative constituents 3-4-5 times while the Legislature is in session. The voter-members review key bills under consideration, heated debates over the bills ensue, and they vote to give Rep. Kelley a notion as to their collective thoughts.
>
> How do I know this to be true? I've been fortunate to serve on the Constituent Advisory Board for each of the past four years. Representative Kelley's action is, in my view, true representation of the people, by the people, and for the people. In Rep. Kelley's mind and actions, people do come before politics! Keep up the good work in listening to and representing all 20,000 constituents of

House District 20! On Tuesday, Nov. 2, please join me in voting for Doris Kelley.

By convening constituent committees, we might find that the American people are less divided than the media and some politicians would have us believe. Whether coming from a "red state" or "blue state," the rural heartland or urban America, the solutions these committees create might be surprisingly similar. That would help Congress to understand that the American people are united behind a particular approach. Or these committees might come up with widely different approaches. One of these might be just the kind of bipartisan solution that Congress had not been able to devise on its own. In either case—a broad consensus among the committees or widely varying approaches—the results might help Congress break out of gridlock.

Most importantly, a network of bipartisan constituent advisory committees throughout the U.S. could help bring civility back to our national politics, by showing that Americans of all political persuasions can sit down together to discuss important issues. It might even be the foundation for a "People's Congress," in which constituent advisory committees from across the U.S. send representatives to a national gathering to attempt to reach consensus on recommendations to Congress on pressing issues.

We Americans are problem-solvers; perhaps all that Congress needs to do is give us some power and step out of the way. Let's encourage members of Congress to move beyond a "go it alone" attitude and embrace a new form of leadership, one more suited to the 21st century, in which teamwork, partnerships, and collaboration are leading the way.

5

CROWD-LEGISLATING

A SIMPLE ACT OF INNOVATION: For politicians to sponsor innovation contests offering financial rewards for the best solutions to our nation's challenges.

The desire of reward is one of the strongest incentives of human conduct.
—Alexander Hamilton

amilton's observation of human nature is as true today as when he wrote it in 1788. The quest for financial reward has fueled creativity, innovation, and imagination in the American marketplace with vigor unmatched anywhere else in the world. Why not similarly unleash the ingenuity of the American people on the political challenges of the nation, through competition and the promise of financial reward?

The power of the "crowd" has transformed our world. Crowdsourcing has unleashed the creativity of millions of people. Crowdfunding has opened up financing for small and large ventures in a wholly new way. It's time that Congress started using the tools of the 21st century. It's time for crowd-legislating.

The idea is simple. Let the American people compete to solve our nation's challenges. Whether for immigration, healthcare, energy, or job creation, let's offer cash prizes for the best political solutions. The internet has sparked the explosive growth of a powerful form of crowd-sourcing: the "innovation contest." Companies have taken to using innovation contests to develop new products and make research breakthroughs. Philanthropies use them to solve pressing social issues. Even some federal agencies have embraced the concept. But the Congress—the place where we really need new ideas—has yet to utilize this 21st century tool. Crowd-legislating would bring the best minds of America into the legislative process itself.

A HISTORY OF CROWDSOURCING

Today's wired-in generation might think that innovation contests are a recent idea, made possible only by the power of the internet. But such contests have actually been around for centuries. Some of the world's most significant advances in public health, safety, and prosperity have resulted from such competitions.

One of the first recorded innovation contests was launched almost 300 years ago. The British government, in 1714, established the "Longitude Prize" to solve the problem of accurately determining a ship's position at sea. Mariners in those times could determine a ship's latitude—distance north or south of the equator—but lacked accurate methods to determine longitude—distance east or west on the globe. The failure to know a ship's true location resulted in the all-too-frequent loss of ships, crews, and cargo. To solve this problem, the British government offered prizes up to twenty thousand British pounds (the equivalent of $3 million today), with the prize amount depending on the accuracy of the solution.

It took almost 60 years, but in 1773 John Harrison won the top prize. A self-taught carpenter with a talent for clock-making, he attacked the problem from a different angle than expected. Most innovators were working to refine the star charts used at sea, but Harrison instead improved the timepieces that were a necessary part of navigation. His ingenuity transformed maritime navigation.

The French government embraced the idea of innovation contests in the early 1700s, as well. In 1721, the French Royal Academy of Sciences launched a series of contests to solve scientific and mathematical problems. Although the winners received medals rather than cash, the prospect of public praise and career advancement proved a powerful incentive for research breakthroughs.

In 1775, the French government began offering cash prizes, with King Louis XVI offering 2,400 French pounds to whoever could create an efficient process to produce alkali, a key ingredient in the manufacture of glass, textiles, soap, and paper. Alkali from natural sources had become increasingly scarce in Western Europe; its importation was expensive. Nicolas Leblanc won the contest in 1791 by inventing an industrial process to produce the needed substance. (In an unfortunate side-note, Leblanc's alkali factory was destroyed in the French Revolution, preventing the King from giving him his reward, and it was sixty years later that his heirs finally received the prize payment from the French government).

Emperor Napoleon Bonaparte continued the contest tradition in 1795 as he turned his attention to conquering Europe. Bonaparte, who considered to have coined the adage that "an army marches on its stomach," offered 12,000 francs to whoever could devise a way to safely preserve food to supply his large army sprawled across the European continent. The prize was won by Nicolas François Appert, for his method of boiling and sealing food in glass bottles. The technique was a great success and, not long after, the British improved it by substituting tin cans for glass bottles, leading to the modern canning industry.

Following those early innovation contests, governments and philanthropists have funded scores of competitions spurring technological breakthroughs. America's first automobile race was held in Chicago in 1895, sponsored by the *Chicago Times-Herald* with a $5,000 prize for "inventors who can construct practicable, self propelling road carriages." In 1919, a prize of $25,000 was offered for the first aviator to fly non-stop between New York and Paris, won eight years later by Charles Lindbergh in the "Spirit of St. Louis" airplane. And in 1996, the highly-publicized "X" prize was offered: $10 million for the first private spaceship able to fly three people to a height of 60 miles twice within two weeks. The prize was won in 2004 by Mojave Aerospace Ventures, whose design was the basis for the spaceship now being developed by Virgin Galactic with the goal of commercializing space travel.

But all of that is old school. With the advent of the internet, new and more powerful ways to harness the knowledge of millions of people have emerged under the banners of crowd-sourcing, open-sourcing, crowd-funding, and the like. Let's explore those next.

THE WISDOM OF THE CROWD

In the 2007 book, *Wikinomics: How Mass Collaboration Changes Everything*, authors Don Tapscott and Anthony D. Williams describe the ways that crowdsourcing and on-line collaboration and competition are revolutionizing the business world. *Wikinomics* opens with the story of Goldcorp Inc., a small Canadian mining company that launched one of the first crowdsourcing efforts of the internet age, turning itself from a failing enterprise into one of the most successful gold-mining companies in the world.

In the late 1990s, Goldcorp was plagued by strikes, debt, and high costs of production. The company's fifty-year-old mine in Red Lake, Ontario had ceased operating, leaving the company with an uncertain future. But in 2000 the company's president, Robert McEwen, at a business conference at the Massachusetts Institute of Technology, learned about Linux, the "open source" computer software developed online by thousands of volunteer programmers. The concept sparked McEwen's imagination. Why not use a similar "open source" approach to locate undiscovered gold at the Red Lake mine?

McEwen launched the *Goldcorp Challenge*. Breaking the mining industry's tradition of secrecy, McEwen posted every possible piece of geological data about the Red Lake mine on its website and offered $575,000 in prize money for the identification of possible hidden deposits of gold. Thousands of people around the world took up the challenge. One hundred and ten locations were identified, of which the overwhelming majority—four out of every five—proved to contain substantial quantities of gold. The company's future was turned around entirely. Battling for its very existence in 2000, Goldcorp's worth has since soared to over $8 billion.

Since then, the use of innovation contests has exploded. No longer just a tool of desperation, as in the case of Goldcorp, the practice is now employed by some of the most successful companies in the world. In 2011, Microsoft offered a prize of $200,000 for the best solution to address computer security threats. That same year, General Electric launched a contest for the best new ideas to improve early detection and diagnosis of breast cancer with prizes of $100,000 for each of the top five ideas.

Innovation contests have become so well-established that firms have emerged with the sole function of deploying them for paying clients. Innocentive and Skild are two such companies now managing hundreds of innovation contests for businesses and public-sector organizations around the world.

Some corporations have used contests not just for profit, but to advance the social good. In 2008, Google created the *Google* 10^{100} contest based on the question: "If you could suggest a unique idea that would help as many people as possible, what would it be?" A fund of $10 million was established to turn the best ideas into reality. Contestants from more than 170 countries submitted over 150,000 ideas, from which Google selected the 16 best ideas for on-line public voting. Five winners were selected advancing on-line education, student robotics, public access to government documents, human powered transportation, and math and science education in Africa.

In 2010, Pepsi launched the *Pepsi Refresh Project*, a $20 million competition to promote social innovation and community development. Pepsi sought proposals in six categories: Arts & Culture, Education, Food & Shelter, Health, the Planet, and Neighborhoods. With over 61 million votes cast on-line to choose the winners, Pepsi awarded grants ranging from $5,000 to $250,000 to hundreds of projects for schools, parks and playgrounds, children's homes, shelters and affordable housing.

An innovation contest tied directly to political problem-solving is the Bloomberg Philanthropies' *Mayors Challenge*, seeking bold solutions to urban problems. Each year, cities compete for a grand prize of $5 million and four additional prizes of $1 million. In the competition's first year, in 2013, over three hundred U.S. mayors submitted proposals.

The first year's grand prize was won by Providence, Rhode Island for a project to improve the young children's vocabularies and enhance their overall academic prospects, through an innovative use of technology. Research shows that children growing up in low-income households hear 30 million fewer words in their first three years than more affluent children. Word exposure is thought to be one of the greatest predictors of future academic achievement. Children in the *Providence Talks* program wear a small recording device with software that measures word count. Based on the recording results, parents are coached on language exposure and vocabulary development, with the goal of closing the "word gap."

Other winners were Houston, using technology to dramatically increase its recycling rate; Chicago, analyzing "big data" to spot hidden trends, so the city can head off problems before they accelerate; and Santa Monica, creating a first-of its kind program in the U.S. that tracks community well-being through a set of key indicators, so the city can best align resources, programs and policies for community improvement.

Interestingly, the fifth winner, Philadelphia, won with an idea that itself uses innovation contests. Called *FastFWD*, Philadelphia's innovation contest addresses public safety. An open call was made for contestants anywhere in the world to propose entrepreneurial approaches to improve public safety. In two rounds, eighteen winners have each been awarded $10,000 and participated in a 12-week impact-accelerator program to improve their ideas' viability and potential impact and scale. They were then eligible for a $100,000 funding pool to pilot their programs in the city. Three startup companies were selected in the first round to receive support from the city for implementation:

Jail Education Solutions, which aims to reduce recidivism and increase post-release employment opportunities through a computer tablet-based self-driven inmate education program.

Textizen, which uses a text-based service to communicate with parolees and/or individuals re-entering society after being in prison.

Village Defense, a high-tech form of "neighborhood watch," which alerts community members of threats via text, phone, or email.

The *Bloomberg Philanthropies' Mayors Challenge* has since held competitions in Europe—where 155 cities in 28 countries participated—and Latin America—where 290 cities in 19 countries participated. In each competition, 20 finalists are chosen by a diverse selection committee and brought together for two days at an "Ideas Camp" to strengthen their proposals through peer feedback and connections to experts.

The prizes enable the winning cities to put their ideas into action, but the benefits go far beyond those cities; other communities around the world are able to learn from their experiences. What's more, the *Mayors Challenge* has found that half of the non-winning finalists have advanced their ideas even in the absence of receiving prizes, spurred by the effort to develop their proposals and their participation in the Ideas Camp.

Another type of civic crowdsourcing is called participatory budgeting. In participatory budgeting, city or town residents develop ideas for how some, or all, of the municipal budget should be spent, and voting then takes place to choose among the various ideas. The approach was invented in the Brazilian city of Porto Alegre in 1989 and has since spread to over a thousand cities worldwide.

Participatory budgeting gained a foothold in the U.S. in 2009 with a program in Chicago that continues today. For years, each Chicago alderman has received over $1 million per year from the city budget for infrastructure improvements in his or her ward. Known locally as "menu money," it goes for street repaving, streetlights, parks and community centers and is spent entirely at the discretion of each alderman. In 2009, Joe Moore, the 4th Ward alderman, decided that ward residents should decide how these funds were to be spent, and he started a four-step process. First, neighborhood meetings were convened at which residents brainstormed ideas for use of the money and volunteers were selected to serve as "community representatives." Next, the community representatives worked together to turn the ideas into proposals for specific projects. Then these proposals were presented to the residents of the ward and refined further based on public input. Finally, community members were invited to attend a ward-wide meeting to vote on which projects to fund.

The projects selected by the community in the first year included sidewalk repairs, bike lanes, a dog park, community gardens, underpass murals, bike racks, benches and shelters at train stations, street paving, solar-powered garbage containers, showers at a public beach, a paved pedestrian path, historical signs and street lighting. Alderman Moore has used participatory budgeting ever since, and in 2013 four more Chicago aldermen pledged to use this approach for their menu money. In 2016, there are now seven wards in Chicago using participatory budgeting.

New York City began a trial program with participatory budgeting in 2011. Like Chicago, each Councilmember receives several million dollars per year for capital improvements. In the first year, four Councilmembers each used participatory budgeting for $1 million of their funds. In 2012, eight Councilmembers used the participatory approach, followed by nine in 2013, and in 2014 nearly half of the Council's 51 members adopted the approach.

Other U.S. cities are experimenting with new variations. Vallejo, California, now uses participatory budgeting city-wide, after its city council voted in 2013 to allocate $2.4 million annually for the effort. And San Francisco, which ran a pilot program in one district in 2013, expanded the program to three districts in 2014, and became the first U.S. city to run its participatory budget process online.

Even some federal agencies have harnessed the power of innovation contests. Since 2010, when the federal government launched *Challenge.gov*, a website for federal innovation contests with cash prizes, more than 80 agencies have run over 600 contests. Over 250,000 people have competed to solve problems such as blocking illegal robocalls, airdropping aid packages in populated areas, and predicting when aging police body armor no longer stops bullets.

There's just one more place we need to unleash the power of innovation contests: the workings of Congress itself. It's time for crowd-legislating. On issue after issue, Congress bogs down in partisan bickering, and none of its members seem able to find a way beyond the impasse. So, instead of relying on the 535 men and women on Capitol Hill to find the answers, or the thousands of lobbyists ready to supply their own, let's look to the more than 300 million Americans.

How It Would Work

Members of Congress would hold contests to solicit ideas from their constituents for solutions to a particular problem. Or they could seek ideas for *any* issue that contestants want them to work on. Members of Congress already have funds that could be used for this. Each member of the House receives approximately $1.25 million per year to maintain offices and staff in Washington and in their districts or states. Senators received around $3.25 million per year for these expenses. Using just a small percentage of those funds—say $20,000—would be enough for a member of Congress to give crowd-legislating a try. If successful, they could allocate up to $100,000 per year—still just a small fraction of their budget—to create an ongoing program.

The contest judges could be the congressional member's staff, their constituent advisory committee (described in Chapter Four), or a bipartisan panel assembled to judge the contest. Entries would be judged on cost-effectiveness, likelihood of success, political feasibility, and other factors. Only new approaches or unique combinations of existing ideas would be eligible to win.

Contest topics could be based on Congressional members' committee assignments. For example, members of the House Subcommittee on Crime, Terrorism, and Homeland Security could hold contests for ways to reduce prison overcrowding, improve port security, or detect terrorist networks. They could hold contests open just to their own constituents, or members of the subcommittee could join together and offer the contests nationwide. By pooling their funds, they could offer sizeable prizes for these national priorities.

The president, as well, could sponsor policy innovation contests. While the Obama White House has made extensive use of on-line tools to receive public input, no cash prizes have been provided. Monetary reward, however, makes all the difference. The current budget for the Executive Office of the President is well over $750 million per year. Allocating just one percent of those taxpayer dollars to innovation contests would provide a prize pool of over $7 million, enough for seven $1 million contests; certainly enough to attract some of America's best thinkers.

The key to successful crowd-legislating is to reward ideas that are not only innovative and effective, but that can gain enough congressional support to be enacted. Excessively partisan ideas—with no chance of passage—are not the goal. One way to achieve this is to have the contest judged by a bipartisan panel. Another is for a portion of the prize money to be awarded only after the winning idea passes Congress. Contestants would thus be motivated to create solutions that can get past the partisan roadblocks.

Let's look at an example of a possible crowd-legislating contest. Consider the problem of America's infant mortality rate, one of the highest of any industrialized country. In 2014, the *Washington Post* reported:

> The United States has a higher infant mortality rate than any of the other 27 wealthy countries, according to a new report from the Centers for Disease Control. A baby born in the U.S. is nearly three times as likely to die during her first year of life as one born in Finland or Japan. That same American baby is about twice as likely to die in her first year as a Spanish or Korean one.

A member of Congress could announce a contest to put the United States in the forefront of infant survival. The contest announcement might read like this:

> Representative Smith invites the public to submit innovative proposals for ways to cut U.S. infant mortality to half of current levels by 2025. Proposals can include roles for the public, private and/or non-profit sectors and include any type of approach or combination of approaches:

medical, educational, nutritional, communications-based, financial, technological, etc. Proposals will be judged on the basis of likelihood of success, cost-effectiveness, achievement of other public health objectives, and achievement of other national objectives. The best proposal, as determined by a bipartisan panel of experts, will receive a prize of $75,000. If the winning proposal is passed by Congress, in substantially the same form, an additional $25,000 will be awarded.

Crowd-legislating contests would not take away the government's authority. The government would always retain the final decision-making power. Crowd-legislating contests would, however, unleash the creative power of America's best thinkers, generating innovative approaches for political leaders to consider. In the example just described, Congressman Smith would have a panel of judges select the best idea, and the Congressman would take it from there, submitting a bill to Congress following the same procedures as if he or his staff had come up with the idea. The difference is that *it just might be a better idea.*

WHAT IF?

Let's examine some political challenges of the recent past that might have benefited from innovation contests. Consider the Iraq war, launched in early 2003. What if the government had offered a large cash prize for the best way to determine if Saddam Hussein possessed suspected Weapons of Mass Destruction (WMDs)? Imagine if America's best thinkers had competed to come up with the fastest and most accurate methods. If the full might of American ingenuity had been applied to that all-important question, might we have discovered that there were, in fact, no WMDs and perhaps have avoided the disastrous Iraq war?

Or if the Iraq war had less to do with WMDs than on deposing Saddam Hussein in order to spread democracy within the region, what if the White House had held a contest for the best way to achieve those goals? New technologies used in creative ways have opened up new possibilities for geopolitical change. In the Arab Spring, Tunisians organized a nationwide uprising using Twitter. The Egyptian revolution was sparked by a Facebook page. Or consider the U.S.'s 2010 Stuxnet cyber-attack on Iran, which deployed a computer virus to disable a sizeable portion of that country's nuclear fuel centrifuges. Applying American innovation to the Iraqi situation might have generated far more effective ideas than the ill-fated military approach that the president and Congress chose.

Consider also the Affordable Care Act ("Obamacare"). The polarization that has resulted from that bill has been intense, even contributing to a partial shutdown of the government in 2013. What if, rather than cobbling together a controversial bill from a hodgepodge of existing ideas, the White House or Congress had unleashed American innovation on the problems facing American healthcare? If the public had been invited to address this challenge, an even better approach, with stronger bipartisan support, might have been found.

Or think about immigration, another challenging issue that Congress can't seem to handle. How can we control our borders? What should we do about the millions of illegal aliens residing in the U.S.? How can we bring in the immigrants that we want— those with smart entrepreneurial ideas, or those willing to work at jobs the rest of won't do, or those fleeing persecution—while keeping out the ones we don't want? Rather than the current battle between the extremes—those who would build a wall around the U.S. versus those who would let in anyone—crowd-legislating could produce creative new ideas from which bipartisan solutions might be found.

TAPPING AMERICA'S POWER OF COMPETITION

In the history of the world, no country has created an economy as successful as that of the U.S. Our gross domestic product now stands at over $17 trillion per year. With all the talk about China's rapid growth, its gross domestic product, at less than $11 trillion, is not even close to ours, even with four times our population. The key to our success? We all know the answer to this question. We learn it in grade school: the power of competition! So let's use that power to help solve America's political challenges.

America's most creative and entrepreneurial-minded people may not be attracted to public office, but we can still enlist them in political problem-solving. The promise of reward has inspired some of the best minds in America to revolutionize computers, the internet, medicine, manufacturing, entertainment, and more. There is no reason why those same imaginative thinkers wouldn't revolutionize policymaking if we offered them similar rewards. It's time we unleashed the power of American ingenuity on our country's problems. It's time for crowd-legislating.

6

No Lying

A Simple Act Of Responsibility: No ideological pledges—
just pledges to results.

Americans are tired of the partisan bickering in Washington, but that doesn't mean we want our politicians to stop fighting for what they (and we) believe in. We just want them to fight *fair*—to follow the same rules we teach our children: not to lie, not to cheat, and not to steal. We want our leaders to serve with integrity. Not just because it's the right thing to do, but because it's the only way to get Washington out of gridlock. This chapter and the next two chapters are based on those simple time-honored rules.

When I say "no lying," I'm not talking about whether politicians are telling the truth about their past, about who they've taken money from, or about who they have or haven't slept with. Of course we want our leaders to be honest, but when it comes to the dysfunction in our democratic institutions, the "lies" I'm talking about are ideological campaign pledges. The classic example is the pledge "no new taxes."

What's wrong with ideological campaign pledges, you might ask? Don't we want—even need—to know what candidates will do once in office? Not if those pledges prevent our leaders from solving our nation's problems, I would argue.

Yes, we need to know what candidates believe in, what they've accomplished, what problems they hope to solve, and what types of approaches they generally favor. But ideological pledges often go too far because they back politicians into a corner, with no room to move. Simplistic pledges that sound good on the campaign trail quickly run up against the complexities of governing once in office. Would a business hire a manager who pledges to never cut prices, or never raise them? To never hire another employee, or never fire one? To never close a factory, or never open a new one? Of course not; smart businesspeople know that the best leaders are those who can adapt to continually changing conditions.

We need members of Congress to acknowledge that the world is complicated, and that circumstances—both at home and abroad—can change quickly and dramatically. We need members of Congress who can respond to those changes without being hamstrung by overly-simplistic ideological pledges. We need members of Congress who have allowed themselves the latitude to negotiate solutions with their fellow lawmakers, without the risk of falling on their ideological swords. And we need members of Congress with the courage to lead, not follow—*leading* one's constituents in a new course of action when the good of the nation requires it, rather than blindly *following* an ill-advised ideological pledge.

Ideological pledges are a symptom of the public's distrust of Congress. When Congress has an approval rating as low as it does today, politicians grasp at anything that will gain them favor. It's understandable; they want to be appreciated as much as the rest of us. Simplistic promises might be seem attractive at first glance, but most Americans understand that such pledges make government function worse, not better. Most Americans don't want pledges to ideology, they want pledges to results. And they expect politicians to be accountable if they are unable to deliver. In Chapter Nine, I describe what those sorts of pledges to results could look like. But the first step is to refrain from ideological pledges.

7

NO CHEATING

A SIMPLE ACT OF INTEGRITY: No filibusters.

I t's ironic that we teach our children to play fair, take turns, and share with others, yet we tolerate the idea that the work of the Senate can be brought to a screeching halt by what, in any other context, might be called bullying: the filibuster!

The filibuster, as a reminder, works like this: any Senator can take the floor and speak for as long as they wish, about anything they wish. As long as they keep this up, the work of the Senate stops. The longest filibuster on record was conducted by Strom Thurmond of South Carolina, who spoke for over 24 hours against the Civil Rights Act of 1957. But that was just the tip of the iceberg; during the nearly three months of deliberations on that bill, nearly two out of every three days were lost to filibusters.

Surprising to some, perhaps, is that the word "filibuster" never appears in the U.S. Constitution. It was not created, nor even anticipated, by the framers. The filibuster is an artifice of congressional rules, about which all the Constitution says is: "Each House may determine its rules of proceedings…"

In the early years of the nation, the Congress operated with no rules limiting debate. Members of the House of Representatives and the Senate could speak for as long as they wished, and no rules were in place to stop a member from dragging out debate indefinitely. While the Congress was small, however, and the scope of federal functions was limited, this was not a problem. But as the Congress's size grew—with the addition of new states and a growing national population—and as the federal government took on more responsibilities, it became clear that limits on speaking time were needed for the Congress to function effectively.

The House of Representatives was the first of the two houses to act. Little more than 50 years after the first Congress, the House had nearly quadrupled in size, growing from an initial 65 members to 242. In response, the House amended its rules in 1841 to state that "no member shall be allowed to speak more than one hour to any question put under debate." To this day, the House has maintained strict limits on the amount of time for debate so that legislative proposals can proceed to a vote.

The Senate was slower to act, in part because its growth was slower. The Senate has taken over 200 years to reach the same quadrupling in size that occurred in the House of Representatives in just over 50 years. The first Senate, convened in 1789, was made up of 24 Senators representing 12 states (Vermont did not ratify the Constitution and apply for admission to the United States until 1791). Today, we have 100 Senators representing 50 states. For well over the first hundred years of the nation, the Senate had no limits on debate. None were needed because until 1900, no more than two dozen filibusters were ever attempted. After the turn of the century, however, the use of filibusters became more common. The situation reached a crisis point in 1917 with a 23-day filibuster against President Woodrow Wilson's efforts to arm merchant ships during the First World War. Wilson was furious, declaring that "the Senate of the United States is the only legislative body in the world which cannot act when its majority is ready for action. A little group of willful men, representing no opinion but their own, have rendered the great government of the United States helpless and contemptible." That same year, in a specially-called session, the Senate passed a new rule to control filibusters. The rule allowed the Senate to invoke what was called "cloture" by which a two-thirds vote of the Senate (lowered to three-fifths in 1975) would force the end of a filibuster.

The filibuster continued to be employed, but up until the 1960s its use was manageable. In a typical two-year congressional term, no more than seven cloture votes were called. But then the floodgates opened. By the end of the 1980s, between twenty and forty cloture votes were being taken in each congressional term. And the number has kept increasing, with over 100 motions for cloture filed in each of the last three Congresses.

But if a filibuster can be ended by a three-fifths vote of the Senate—60 members—what's the problem? It would seem easy to bring a filibuster to a halt. The answer lies in the fact that for the past 37 years, while sometimes the Democrats have held the majority and sometimes the Republicans, those majorities have been slim; neither party has held the 60 or more Senate seats needed to end a filibuster. Thus, whichever party has been in the minority at the time has been able to increasingly use the filibuster to stop the majority from getting things done.

Some people defend the filibuster on the grounds that it "protects the minority." But it's one thing to give the minority party a voice in the debate; it's another give it a veto. And that is what today's use of the filibuster has done. If the founders had intended to require a 60% majority for legislation to pass the Senate, they would have written the Constitution differently. But that's *not* what they intended. They intended legislation to be debated and then put to a majority vote.

It is instructive to consider the origin of the word "filibuster." It sounds so quaint. Probably the name of some portly English gentleman in the British House of Commons, with a reputation for being long-winded, right? Jeremiah K. Filibuster?

Far from it. Filibuster comes from the Spanish word for pirate, *filibustero*, which itself comes from the Dutch word for pirate, *vrijbuiter*, meaning "freebooter." Pirates—men who pillaged and plundered and terrorized the high seas. Men who operated beyond the reach of the law. We might think about that the next time the Congress is held hostage by a filibuster and call the process by its rightful name, piracy.

I am not saying the Senate should abandon the filibuster entirely; some people consider the filibuster to be an act of courage. But I believe it would be just as great an act of courage, perhaps even greater, for members of the Senate to pledge to both abstain from using the filibuster themselves and to vote to end any filibuster attempted by others *until it is properly reformed*. And that reform should be simple, so that the American people have trust in it. Why not simply say that each party gets five filibusters per year? That's slightly more than was the norm up until the 1960s. This reform could be done with a simple change to the Senate rules; no legislation or Constitutional amendment is required. It could even be done through a "gentleman's agreement' between the two parties, with no rule change needed at all.

It is time we returned to the democracy that the founders intended, in which our leaders engage in honest, spirited and principled debate, then vote on the bill in question and let the majority rule.

8

No Stealing

A Simple Act Of Honesty: No earmarks.

Remember the "bridge to nowhere"—the planned $398 million bridge in Alaska that was the subject of controversy in the 2008 presidential election? Hundreds of millions of U.S. taxpayer dollars were to be spent to connect the town of Ketchikan (population 14,000) with 50 residents and the town airport on Gravina Island, despite perfectly adequate ferry service. The bridge was a pet project of Alaska's congressional delegation, to be funded primarily through a federal earmark. With a span nearly as long as the Golden Gate Bridge, and a height surpassing the Brooklyn Bridge, the "bridge to nowhere" would have carried less than 1% of the traffic of either of those other bridges. The bridge became an icon of "pork-barrel politics."

Earmarks, according to the U.S. Office of Management and Budget, are "funds provided by the Congress for projects, programs, or grants...[that circumvent] otherwise applicable merit-based or competitive allocation processes..." Unlike the usual budget allocation process, in which each federal agency receives an annual sum to be spent according to its authorized functions and priorities, earmarks direct taxpayer funds to specific projects, usually in the sponsoring lawmaker's district or state.

Defenders of earmarks point out that while projects like the "bridge to nowhere" may waste hundreds of millions of dollars, amounts such as these are just a fraction of the federal budget. While true, the damage earmarks cause to the functioning of our democracy goes far beyond just the waste of taxpayer dollars. Earmarks erode Americans' trust in the government to spend taxpayer dollars fairly and efficiently. And while earmarks are legal, they are tempting targets for bribes and kickbacks, which clearly are *not* legal. Many corruption cases involving members of Congress have resulted from illegal activity associated with earmarks.

But the problem with earmarks goes even deeper. Earmarks distort the electoral processes at the heart of our democracy, because even when done entirely legally, members of Congress use them to reward supporters and to win votes, giving incumbents a decidedly unfair advantage over challengers. Voters are more likely to overlook failings of their members of Congress, as long as those members bring dollars home to their district.

The effect is that earmarks encourage the electorate to vote based on short-term gain, rather than the ability of a legislator to be an effective participant in solving our nation's problems. An oft-repeated quote, usually ascribed (although likely incorrectly) to Alexis de Tocqueville, is that "the American Republic will endure, until politicians realize they can bribe the people with their own money." Ironically, this makes earmarks one of the few areas of common ground between Democrats and Republicans: "You support my pork-barrel project and I'll support yours, and we'll both be re-elected."

A number of current and former members of Congress, from both parties, have taken stands against the use of earmarks, including leaders like Sen. John McCain (R-AZ), Sen. Russ

Feingold (D-WI), Rep. Michele Bachmann (R-MN) and Rep. John Boehner (R-OH). Since 2011, Congress has operated with a virtual ban on earmarks, led by congressional Republicans and supported by President Obama.

However, that ban is eroding. In the budget bill that ended the October 2013 government shutdown, nearly $3 billion was earmarked for a dam project in Senate Minority Leader Mitch McConnell's home state of Kentucky. And in the 2014 federal funding bill, a number of members of Congress claimed credit for bringing home the bacon, even if the projects weren't technically earmarks. For example, Senator Jerry Moran (R-KS) touted his role in securing $404 million to build the National Bio and Agro-Defense Facility in his home state. Sen. Mary Landrieu (D-LA) took credit for $310 million to construct six Coast Guard cutters in her state, even though the Obama administration had sought funding for just two of those ships and House Republicans sought only four. And several members of Ohio's delegation have championed the spending of almost half a billion dollars for the Abrams tank, despite the Army's chief of staff saying the money would be better spent on other priorities. Why is the Ohio delegation pushing to fund this tank that the Army doesn't want? Because the nation's only tank factory is in their state.

It is sometimes said that earmarks make it easier for Congress to pass legislation, by essentially "buying" the votes of reluctant members. If this is true, I would argue that an alternative to continuing the ban on earmarks would be to use them to their utmost advantage, not just to pass small pieces of legislation, but as an incentive to address big issues.

Here's what I mean: since politicians are so fond of earmarks, why not create a "grand bargain" in which Congress would be allowed to use earmarks as long as it passes a balanced federal budget? As part of this bargain, the earmark process would have to be reformed, to include greater transparency, more equitable allocation of funding amongst districts and states, and involvement of the public in determining the uses and receivers of earmarks. The earmark process could use the principles of participatory budgeting, described in Chapter Seven, giving the public a voice in how earmarks are spent. If we could make the earmark process fair and efficient *and* also balance the federal budget, that would be a "win-win" for the American people and Congress. So a simple act of integrity would be for members of Congress to either reject the use of earmarks entirely or to support their use only when Congress is able to pass a balanced budget.

9

Do Or Die
Responsibility for Results, not Rhetoric

A Simple Pledge Of Accountability: "I will step down from office after two terms (for Senators) or three terms (for Representatives) unless Congress gains at least a 50% public approval rating."

The way to get members of Congress to work together is quite simple: make their right to run for re-election dependent on it! How? Through a vote on Congress, *as a whole*. Only if Congress won this vote of approval, would its members be eligible for re-election. With this one simple change, we would see a new spirit of cooperation in Washington. You see, although we are told that elections hold the politicians accountable to the voters, it's not entirely true. If the American people could actually "throw the bums out" that would be one thing. But the way our elections work, we can only throw our *own* bums out—our own two Senators and one Representative.

What if we had the right to truly throw the bums out—all of them? What if the American people could vote on the entire Congress, not just its individual members? After all, with Congress's approval rating typically barely much above 10 percent, why should *any* member of Congress be allowed to keep his or her seat? If a company's products got a 10 percent approval rating, how long would that company stay in business? And yet Congress, with an approval rating sometimes as low as the single digits, sees its members re-elected at rates topping 90 percent. Election to Congress has become, for all intents and purposes, election for life. Two centuries after we threw off the shackles of the British king, our Congress—the heart of our democracy—has essentially devolved back to a monarchy.

Consider the case of Congressman John Dingell, Jr., who retired from Congress in 2014 after serving over 59 years in office. Not only was he the longest serving member of Congress ever, but he began his congressional career by succeeding his own father, John Dingell, Sr., who had represented the 16th District of Michigan for 22 years. And when Congressman Dingell stepped down in 2014, who succeeded him? His own wife, now Congresswoman Debbie Dingell! How long must a family hold a congressional seat before they are considered royalty?

The problem stems from a basic fact of political systems (and perhaps most human systems): that those who come into positions of power—even when well-intentioned—figure out ways, over time, to use the system to retain that power. Incumbents, who are in those positions of power, have come to enjoy significant advantages over challengers. Congressional committee assignments are increasingly used by incumbents to raise funds from special interests. Modern media gives incumbents far more visibility. The relatively recent emergence of "constituent service" (helping constituents navigate the intricacies of federal agencies and regulations) as a central function of congressional activity lets incumbents curry favor with voters and donors. The same goes for the use of earmarks to fund projects that may be wasteful, but bring spending and jobs to the incumbent's constituents. The three-day congressional workweek and the speed of modern transportation allow incumbents to spend much of their time campaigning at home. And, of course, gerrymandering has, over time, made nearly every congressional district in the country a guaranteed win for one of the two parties.

Given the advantages that incumbents enjoy over challengers, it is no wonder that incumbent re-election rates over the past 40 years have consistently topped 90 percent (with the exception of the elections of 2010, when they dipped to around 85 percent) despite the approval rating of Congress being routinely below 20 percent and often below 10 percent. Re-election has become disconnected from results.

So I propose a new way of voting that would solve all the problems that have accumulated over two centuries, in order to make Congress perform like never before: a nationwide vote on the Congress as a whole, to be held in advance of the general election. If the Congress failed to receive at least 50 percent approval, then every one of its members would be barred from running for re-election. I call this a "performance-based term limit." As long as the Congress performs to the public's satisfaction, no term limit is applied; if the Congress fails to perform, the term limit is applied to them all.

Now, while some readers may be excited at the chance to fire a failing Congress, that is not the goal of this approach. It is just the opposite: to make members of Congress so fearful of losing their jobs that they do everything possible to achieve results for the American people.

Consider how these performance-based term limits would change politicians' mindsets. From their first day in office, they would be focused on working together, because the thing they care about most—holding onto power—would depend on it. They would know that the days of nearly guaranteed re-election are over, because without results to show, there would not be a chance for re-election.

The beauty of the performance-based term limit is that while it would force members of Congress to work together, they couldn't just abandon their partisan allegiances. Passing the "50 percent test" wouldn't mean congressional members automatically get to keep their seats. It would just mean they get to run for re-election. To win re-election, just as now, they would need to convince their partisan base they had advanced their party's causes. As a consequence, members of Congress would be forced to maintain a delicate balance between cooperation and competition. Cooperating with their opponents to accomplish results while, at the same time, competing to promote their partisan principles. That balance is just what is needed to make Congress an effectively performing body.

Of course, changing our voting methods to implement congressional performance-based term limits would take time to achieve. It might even require changing the Constitution (although that is not certain, as I explain later). But in keeping with the spirit of this book's call for individual action, individual members of Congress can start us down this path. All they need to do is make a simple pledge: to step down from office after a set time if the Congress as a whole cannot achieve a 50 percent approval rating in public opinion polls. Why not three terms for Representatives (six years) and two terms for Senators (twelve years)? What could be more courageous for a politician than to pledge to "do or die"?

THE FAILURE OF THE DEMOCRATIC MARKETPLACE

Opponents of term limits often say: "we already have term limits; they are called elections." But the idea that voting separates the wheat from the chaff is a myth. The elections of 2008 were a particularly striking example. The U.S. was five years into a seemingly endless and disastrous war; we were free-falling into the worst economic crash since the Great Depression; barely one in ten Americans approved of Congress's performance; and both presidential candidates cloaked themselves in the mantle of "change." Yet the American people overwhelmingly sent the same old members of Congress back to Washington. Not a single one of the 27 Senate incumbents seeking re-election lost a primary race, and only 4 lost in the general election (and one of those four lost presumably because he was a recently convicted felon!). In the House of Representatives, out of the 404 incumbents running for re-election, only 4 lost their primary races, and in the general election only 19 lost their seats. In an election so dominated by calls for change, how did roughly nine out of ten incumbents return to Washington to reclaim their seats at the tables of power?

While the election results of 2008 may have been particularly distressing, they were far from unusual. Since the founding of our nation, congressional re-election rates have been shockingly high, topping 80 percent in nearly three-fourths of all elections, and rarely falling below 70 percent in the remainder. Since 1968, the problem has gotten even worse, with re-election rates exceeding 90 percent in all but 4 out of 22 congressional elections. The 2012 elections continued this pattern, with 90 percent of House incumbents and 91 percent of Senate incumbents retaining their seats. In the 2014 elections, an astonishing 95 percent of congressional incumbents running for re-election won their races.

At the same time re-election rates have been rising, so too have the rates at which members of Congress choose to put themselves up for re-election. It has not always been so. In the early years of our democracy, the notion of a career politician did not exist. Most

Americans held the view that politics was a vile affair; public service was to be done quickly, after which one would happily return to private life.

While that attitude changed with the rise of political careerism in the 1800s, another force kept incumbency in check: party solidarity. Members of Congress often stepped down to give others in their party a chance, either voluntarily or under pressure from the party bosses. Abraham Lincoln exemplified this attitude when, after serving a single term in the House of Representatives, he declined to run for re-election stating that "to enter myself as a competitor of another…is what my word and honor forbid." During the seven decades between 1824 and 1896, in a typical election, one out of every three members of the House of Representatives would decline to run for re-election. This trend reached a high point in the election of 1842, when well over half of the House of Representatives chose not to run for re-election.

By the late 1800s the code among politicians of "I had my turn, now it's your turn" began to deteriorate, for a number of reasons. With the rise of the "professional class" in America, the electorate developed a greater tolerance for "professional politicians." The emergence of permanent congressional committees, chaired by seniority, created a greater incentive to remain in office. The switch to direct primaries from closed-door party nominating conventions took away the power of the party leadership to select candidates. And the growth in size and complexity of the federal government made a compelling argument that extended tenure in office was necessary for the effective functioning of government. For all of these reasons, incumbents sought re-election at ever-higher rates. By the 1940s, typically 90 percent of House incumbents sought to retain their seats and the rate has remained at that level, or higher, since.

By the 1990s, the situation had gotten quite extreme, with incumbents nearly always seeking re-election and winning almost 100 percent of the time. The average tenure of a member of Congress was over 10 years, nearly as long as the average tenure of lifetime-appointed Supreme Court Justices. Congressional turnover was nearly entirely dependent on members resigning, running for higher office, or dying. In reaction, 23 states adopted laws imposing term limits on their members of Congress. But in 1995, voting five to four, the Supreme Court ruled these laws unconstitutional. Around that same time, several constitutional amendments to impose congressional term limits were introduced in the House of Representatives, but only one managed to obtain even a bare majority of votes, far short of the two-thirds required for passage.

But traditional term limits, even if we could impose them, provide no guarantee of fixing the problems with Congress. The problem is not that lawmakers remain in office too long; it's that they don't accomplish anything while there. Simply replacing incumbents with newcomers, without any additional incentives for results, might achieve nothing. Fixed term limits could actually make the problems worse, by removing what little accountability there is and encouraging candidates who favor stonewalling over action. What the voters want is performance, regardless of how long a person serves. Perhaps that's why less than a third of all U.S. states have term limits for state legislators, despite such limits *at the state level* being allowable under the U.S. Constitution.

The fact is that there is a fundamental flaw at the heart of our system of representative democracy. What the framers of the Constitution failed to anticipate is this: while the Congress's job is to manage the affairs of the nation as a whole, the electoral processes set up by the Constitution provide *individual* members of

Congress with little, if any, incentive to work toward that end. Instead, our electoral system rewards those who act primarily for the narrow parochial interests of their districts and states or who toe a rigid party line. That, more than anything, is why we have the gridlock in Washington today: our system of democracy lacks any means to hold members of Congress accountable to the national electorate as a whole. In the absence of such electoral accountability, it is perhaps understandable, although regrettable, why Congress's performance consistently fails to meet the expectations of the American people.

Interestingly enough, America's local governments faced this same problem in the early days of our nation and solved it with an electoral innovation that exists to this day: at-large representation. Prior to the American Revolution, local governments played fairly limited roles. During the 1800s, however, town and city governments grew rapidly as they were called upon to provide new public services: police and fire protection, education, trash collection, road construction and repair, and the like. But the structures of local government were ill-equipped to properly discharge these functions. At the root of the problem was the ward system of government.

At the time, nearly all local governments operated under what is known as the ward, or district, structure, in which the locality is divided up into different areas, each of which elects a member to the municipal council. By the late 1800s, the flaws in this system were becoming apparent. Councilors often seemed indifferent to the needs of the city or town as a whole, caring only about their narrow neighborhood interests. What's more, the system was a breeding ground for corruption. Municipal councils had the responsibility to award lucrative contracts for public services—streetcars, telephone, gas and electric franchises—and the opportunities for bribery were many. Yet as long as councilors paid patronage to the power-brokers in their districts and ensured that funds were spent there—no matter how wastefully—they continued to be voted back into office. New York City's aldermen earned the nickname the "Forty Thieves," while a crooked group of Chicago councilors were known as the "Gray Wolves."

(Does this sound like the Congress of today, in which the exorbitant cost of running for office entices members to put narrow or parochial interests ahead of the good of the nation as a whole?)

To address these problems, America's cities and towns increasingly adopted the idea of "at-large" representation, whereby councilors were elected by the populace as a whole, rather than a single ward or district. The idea spread throughout the country and today the overwhelming majority of U.S. city councils (66 percent) include some form of at-large representation. Most often, city councils include both at-large and ward-elected councilors. This ensures that the government is accountable to individual districts of the city—including minority-dominated neighborhoods—as well as to the community as a whole.

Congress, of course, still operates under the same type of district system that caused cities and towns so much trouble, with members of the House of Representatives being elected by district and members of the Senate being elected by state. *Not a single member of Congress is accountable to the nation as a whole!* Could Congress take the same course of action as America's cities and towns, by having some members elected by the entire nation? It's an idea worth considering.

Imagine the Senate expanded by just ten at-large members, each to be elected by the entire American electorate. These additional senators, accountable to the whole nation, might be enough to dramatically improve the workings of the Senate. For example, these at-large senators might be more inclined than most to vote for cloture to end a filibuster, enabling the Senate to get on with its work. Holding national elections for these posts would be manageable because, given the staggered senatorial terms of six years, there would only be three or four at-large seats to fill every two years. Imagine a national race every two years in which the top three or four finishers win the seats in the Senate. This might bring disaffected voters back into the electoral process and it could even open the door to viable candidates from third parties.

The House of Representatives is a different story. For at-large seats to make a difference, they would similarly need to constitute at least 10 percent of the House's total. But with 435 voting members of the House—all with 2 year terms—this would mean 44 at-large seats up for nationwide vote at the same time every 2 years. Between Democrats, Republicans, and independents, there could be more than 130 candidates running. That would be far too much for the voters to keep track of.

Performance-based term limits, however, avoid all of the complications of at-large congressional seats. Accountability to the whole nation would be achieved with just a simple yes-or-no vote on whether Congress has done well enough that incumbents should have the chance to run for re-election. And performance-based term limits have other advantages over at-large seats. They make the *entire* Congress accountable to the nation at-large, not just some of its members, while at the same time retaining accountability to the constituents "back home," because candidates still must compete in their district or state races. And whereas at-large elections can be won by style over substance, a vote on the Congress as a whole would be based on results, because it would be a vote for an institution as a whole, not an individual.

Make no mistake about it: members of Congress *will* produce results if we give them a reason to do so. While Congress as an institution might appear incompetent, many of its members are not. These 535 men and women hold the most coveted positions of power in the world; winning those seats required cunning and tenacity. By instilling in them the fear of losing their seats, these 535 people could turn the Congress into one of the most powerful problem-solving institutions on the planet.

Incentives drive behavior. That is a fact of life. President Lincoln famously orated in his first inaugural address that "the mystic chords of memory...will yet swell the chorus of the Union, when again touched...by the better angels of our nature." Unfortunately, Lincoln was wrong and the Civil War was the result. The better angels of our nature are rarely to be found in politics. Saints may work solely for the common good, but we mortals will always be driven by a measure of self-interest. Rare are the men or women who run for Congress *solely* for the good of the country or the betterment of their constituents. They also like the power and perks. So let's use those desires to our advantage.

A performance-based term limit would harness politicians' desire for power. Most of them begin planning their re-election as soon as they take office. A performance-based term limit wouldn't change that; it would take advantage of it. As soon as they were sworn in, the members of Congress, no matter how divided politically, would be forced to sit down together and plan how to meet the needs of the electorate. They would be forced to figure out which issues matter most to the voters. They would be forced to determine how the two parties differ on those issues, and devise ways they might resolve those differences.

Performance-based term limits would wrest control of our government from the lobbyists and wealthy donors. I'm not saying that politicians would stop thinking about raising money for their campaigns or paying attention to lobbyists. But they'd be well aware that first and foremost they'd better please the broad electorate, because if they failed to get the required 50 percent approval to run for re-election, all the money and lobbyists in the world wouldn't matter.

THE PATH TO PERFORMANCE-BASED TERM LIMITS

But wouldn't performance-based term limits require changing the Constitution? If applied to the whole Congress, the answer is possibly yes, so let's first call on politicians to adopt performance-based term limits as individual pledges: to step down after one term (for Senators) or three terms (for Representatives) unless Congress can obtain a 50 percent public approval rating.

Voluntary term limit pledges are not a new idea. In recent years, some candidates to Congress have made pledges to the traditional form of term limits, promising to step down after a set number of terms. Senator Sam Brownback, a Kansas Republican, stepped down after two terms in 2011, honoring the pledge he had made. Congresswoman Helen Chenoweth, an Idaho Republican, honored her pledge to serve no more than three terms in the House, stepping down in 2000.

A variation of performance-based term limit could be individual pledges based on specific goals. Steve Moak, a congressional candidate from Arizona, demonstrated this type of accountability in 2010 by pledging to step down if Congress failed to balance the federal budget within six years of his taking office. Moak said "In the business world, people are held accountable for results, and it should be no different in Congress. This pledge is a real and measurable commitment to the people of [Congressional

District 3]. If the budget isn't balanced in six years, I'm out of a job. No gimmicks, no fine print."

What are some other goals that candidates could pledge to accomplish, with a promise to step down if unreached by a certain time? Cutting the federal debt in half? Passing an immigration reform bill? Raising the high school graduation rate to 95 percent? Achieving energy independence? Reducing crime?

Another pathway to implementing congressional performance-based term limits would be for individual states to adopt them. This could be done without any changes to the Constitution. How could that be, you might ask? Surely this new form of election would require constitutional reform; after all, enacting term limits on the presidency required the passage of the Twenty-Second Amendment. And in 1995, the U.S. Supreme Court ruled that congressional term limits are unconstitutional, striking down laws in the 23 states that had enacted them.

Performance-based term limits are different, however. Unlike a fixed term limit, which doesn't give the voters any say about whether an incumbent may run again or not, performance-based term limits would give the voters a voice. Let me give an example. Let's say a state adopted performance-based term limits for its members of Congress. Before the primaries are even held, the voters of that state would be given the chance to vote with a single "yes or no" ballot on whether their entire federal delegation, as a whole, had performed well enough that they should be allowed to run for re-election. If they failed to get at least a 50 percent "yes" vote, then none of them would be eligible to run. Then the state would proceed with primaries, as usual, for the parties to select their nominees. So the performance-based term limit vote would just be part of the overall primary process.

While the Constitution provides the framework for general elections for Congress, it is silent on primaries. Primaries only came into being as a way for political parties to choose their candidates. At the time of the drafting of the Constitution, there *were* no political parties. And despite the emergence of parties soon after the ratification of the Constitution, more than a century passed before primaries came into being. Through the end of the 1800s, candidates were chosen by party leaders, often behind closed doors. Primaries arose during the Progressive era of the early 1900s, in reaction to the control of the nominating process by party leaders. So, because of the Constitution's silence on primaries, states have the right to determine their structure, within certain bounds.

To illustrate the latitude that states have in deciding who gets to run in the general election, it should be noted that nearly every state has some form of "sore loser law" barring candidates who lose in the primary from running in the general election as independents. California goes so far as to bar candidates from running in the general election as independents purely on the basis of being affiliated with a political party in the year prior to the primary, regardless of whether they ran in the primary or not. These laws have been found by the courts to be constitutional. So perhaps it might be allowable for an individual state to give its voters the right to bar their current members of Congress from running for re-election, on the basis of a statewide vote on their collective performance.

But what about the Supreme Court's 1995 ruling that states may not impose term limits on their members of Congress? The relevant issue is that the Court's ruling objected to absolute term limits, in other words, based on a *fixed* amount of time. Performance-based term limits are different. They are not absolute.

They are conditional. Despite the name I have given them—performance-based term limits—they might not be term limits at all from a constitutional perspective, but rather ballot access requirements, in the same way that candidates must obtain a certain number of signatures to run in the primary or general election. If it is constitutional to require a show of "legitimacy" by obtaining signatures (and the Supreme Court *has* found it constitutional), then it might be similarly allowable to require a candidate to demonstrate legitimacy by being part of a Congress that has majority public support.

It also should be noted that for nearly 200 years, states *did* have the right to impose term limits on their members of Congress. It was only in 1995 that the Supreme Court ruled against them. And that ruling was closely divided with a five-to-four vote. The dissenting opinion in that case stated: "Nothing in the Constitution deprives the people of each State of the power to prescribe eligibility requirements for the candidates who seek to represent them in Congress. The Constitution is simply silent on this question. And where the Constitution is silent, it raises no bar to action by the States or the people." It is entirely possible that a future Supreme Court would find performance-based term limits constitutional.

But there is an easier pathway to begin experimenting with performance-based term limits and that is by looking to the traditional "laboratories of democracy": the states and local communities. From among the nearly 20,000 cities and towns in the U.S., there must be some that would be willing, even eager, to try this new and more accountable approach to democracy. There may also be states ready to try performance-based term limits for their state legislatures; after all, nearly a third of all states already have fixed term limits for their legislatures. The advantage of working at these levels of government is that in many cities and towns, a change to the municipal charter to adopt this method can be done by a petition of the citizens, and the same is true in a number of states for changes to their state constitutions.

I admit that this is an experiment. We don't really know how the system I propose would play out in practice. Perhaps people would be reluctant to vote against Congress as a whole, if it meant they would also be throwing out their own incumbents. After all, it is common wisdom that while we may detest Congress, we like our own incumbents. On the other hand, if your current representative and senators are not to your liking, you might be more inclined to vote against the Congress as a whole. For those concerned that this approach doesn't give incumbents who are truly competent the chance to remain, it is worth pointing out that if Congress failed its performance test, the incumbents thrown out would only have to sit out one term. They would then be free to run in the next election cycle to try to win back their seat.

There are doubtlessly variations to what I propose. Perhaps Congress should be given more of a chance, with at least 60 percent of the voters disapproving before incumbents lose their eligibility for re-election. Perhaps rather than all incumbents losing the right to run for re-election in the case of a vote of disapproval, it would only be those who had been in office for a certain length of time. Perhaps there should be an override, in which individual members could run in the primaries even if Congress failed its overall vote, but they would have to win at least 75% of the primary vote to then run in the general election. Perhaps, rather than every two years, there would just be a "clean sweep" vote at longer intervals, say every eight years. In this scenario, with an up-or-down vote on the entire Congress at eight-year intervals, a vote of disapproval would result in *every* member being barred from running for re-election, regardless of how many terms they had served. Do you have ideas about how performance-based term limits should be done? I invite readers to go to www.fromoathtoaction.com and suggest different approaches.

But there is no need to wait to start down this road of reform. We can begin just one politician at a time. By taking an individual oath to step down within a set number of terms unless a specific goal is reached—whether that is a 50 percent approval rating of all Americans or a specific measurable result like a balanced budget—members of Congress can show they have the courage to be accountable to the American people—all of us.

PART II

★★★

THE PRESIDENT

10

ONE PERSON, ONE VOTE, ONE NATION

A PRESIDENTIAL PLEDGE OF FAIRNESS: "If I should win the Electoral College, but lose the popular vote, I will offer my opponent a role in my administration."

Every four years, the nation decries the failings of the so-called Electoral College. Untold numbers of Americans stay home on Election Day, convinced their votes make no difference. Yet despite two centuries of efforts to abolish this system—over 700 bills introduced in Congress—the Electoral College survives intact to this day.

So it's time to take a different approach. It's time to be practical. This chapter's act of courage—a pledge by each presidential candidate that should they win the Electoral College, but lose the popular vote, they will offer their opponent a role in leading the nation—could fix many of the problems of the current system and just might be the stepping stone toward the Electoral College's eventual abolition.

This pledge requires no changes to the Constitution or passage of legislation. It requires nothing more than an act of courage by just two Americans. Nothing more than a simple, yet bold, promise that the will of the people should count for something.

With this simple pledge, our democracy would be transformed. Millions of disengaged voters would finally have a reason to come to the polls. The candidates would begin campaigning with an eye toward the interests of all Americans, not just the swing voters in the swing states. And perhaps most importantly, the public's trust in our government would be renewed by the candidates' commitment to make every vote count.

While this proposal may seem radical on its face—a voluntary sharing of power—there is, in fact, a long history of such conciliatory gestures. Nearly every one of the last ten presidents has brought at least one member of the opposing party into his administration to demonstrate post-election bipartisanship, typically as a Cabinet secretary and once as the United Nations ambassador. John F. Kennedy, after his 1960 victory over Richard Nixon in the closest election in nearly 50 years, did, in fact, offer Nixon a role in his administration (at least temporarily), although Nixon chose to decline. Abraham Lincoln, seeing the need for unity in a time of national crisis, brought his foremost rivals for the presidential nomination into his cabinet in the first term of his presidency.

Regardless of one's feelings about the presidential candidates— and at this time, in the midst of a presidential election, such feelings are strong—the fact remains that a candidate who has won the support of a majority of the voting public is clearly in touch with the sentiments of a sizeable portion of the American electorate. Not only would the duly-elected president demonstrate a commitment to fairness by offering their opponent a role in their administration, they would benefit by having someone on their team who can be a liaison to those constituencies and provide an understanding of their hopes and fears. That would be a valuable service both to the president's administration and to the American people.

I acknowledge that, much as it would be an honorable gesture for the duly-elected president to give his or her opponent a role running an arm of the government or representing the United States as an ambassador or diplomat, they simply might not feel that the opponent's skills match those positions. They might want to create a role more like a special advisor to the president. If nothing else, the president could make a commitment to meet with their opponent on a regular basis to hear his or her views on the nation's challenges and have a respectful discussion about strategies to meet them.

Frankly, any president would be wise to meet occasionally with their electoral opponent, even those presidents who have won both the Electoral College *and* the popular vote. It would help them stay in touch with the broad range of political perspectives. The president would be under no obligation to heed the opponent's advice. But the president might, in fact, be surprised by the outcomes that result by bringing their different viewpoints together.

So a variation of this pledge could be to state: "If I am elected, I will invite my opponent to sit down with me periodically to share his/her views, and in the 'highly improbable event' that I am not elected, I will be willing to do the same." A pledge like this, I would argue, does not require much courage at all; just an open-minded approach to serving the nation.

WHAT HAPPENED TO DEMOCRACY?

When people talk about the Electoral College, they often ask what happened to "one person, one vote"? Doesn't the Constitution guarantee us that right? Isn't that at the heart of our democracy?

The fact is that nowhere in the Constitution do the words "one person, one vote," or anything approximating it, appear. In fact, the Constitution is quite clear that the *states*, not the people, elect the president and vice president. The Constitution directs each state to appoint "electors," who are to meet in their respective state capitols in early December, to cast *their* votes for president and vice president. Each state's results are then sent to the President of the Senate, and a joint session of Congress is held on January 6, at which time the votes are counted and the winners of the election are declared.

But wait a minute, some might say, the states appoint the electors? What about Election Day when *we* vote for the president and vice president? Where does that fit in?

The fact is that on Election Day, we are not voting in a single national election and we are not actually voting for the president and vice president. What actually takes place are 50 separate elections to choose each state's electors. The fact that the presidential and vice presidential candidates' names are on the ballot is purely informational. For example, New York State's election law reads: "Each vote cast for the candidates of any party or independent body for president and vice president of the United States and each vote cast for any write-in candidates for such offices shall be deemed to be cast for the candidates for elector of such party..." And who decides who those "candidates for elector" will be? The leaders of each state's political parties.

What's more, while we take for granted the right to vote for those electors, that right is not, in fact, guaranteed anywhere in the Constitution. The Constitution leaves it entirely up to each state to decide how to appoint its electors, stating (italics added): "Each State shall appoint, *in such Manner as the Legislature thereof may direct*, a Number of Electors, equal to the whole Number of Senators and

Representatives to which the State may be entitled in the Congress…"

As far as the Constitution is concerned, a state could choose its electors by having its legislature play pin-the-tail-on-the-donkey (or elephant, to be fair). In the early days of the nation, many state legislatures actually *did* choose the electors themselves, without any vote by the citizens. It was only over time that the states gave the right to choose electors to the citizens.

The "winner takes all" method of elections, used by all but two states, is not mandated by the Constitution either. In the "winner takes all" method, the presidential candidate receiving the most votes gets all of that state's electors, regardless of whether he or she won by one or a million votes. In fact, a candidate doesn't even have to get a majority of the state's votes to be awarded all of the state's electors. Take, for instance, the 1992 presidential election, in which Ross Perot ran as a strong third-party candidate, drawing significant votes in nearly all states. Despite no candidate winning a majority of votes in any state except Arkansas (and the District of Columbia), every single state's electoral votes went entirely to one of the two major party candidates. In fact, in eight states, the winning candidate did not receive even 40 percent of the votes cast, yet because of the "winner take all" system, he received all of the state's electoral votes.

THE PROBLEMS WITH THE ELECTORAL COLLEGE

So what are the problems with the Electoral College? Why should we trouble ourselves with fixing it? After all, some would argue that the system works just fine. Such proponents, however, are in the minority; most Americans consider the Electoral College to be undemocratic. What's more, it brings with it a host of other problems. Let's explore what those problems are.

INEQUALITY

At its core, the Electoral College violates Americans' belief in equality. The Declaration of Independence may proclaim "that all men are created equal" but our votes for president are not; some Americans' votes carry more weight than others.

The Constitution allots each state a number of electors equal to the number of its senators and representatives in the Congress. Because every state has two senators, regardless of population, less-populated states get more electors per resident than more heavily-populated states. If we compare the smallest and largest states, the inequality is glaring. Wyoming has around 584,000 residents and 3 electoral votes, giving the state one electoral vote for every 195,000 residents. California, with nearly 40 million residents and 55 electoral votes, receives one electoral vote for every 709,000 residents. The result is that a Wyoming voter has nearly four times more say in the election of the president than a Californian. Compared to California, the motto of Wyoming voters could be "One person, four votes"!

CYNICISM & APATHY

Perhaps the most apparent problems with the Electoral College system are the cynicism and diminished voter turnout it breeds. In states where the presidential outcome is a near-certainty due to the historical dominance of one party over the other, voters are less inclined to vote.

California and Wyoming, once again, are good examples of this problem. Wyoming has given its electoral votes to the Republican candidate in every election for the past 50 years. California has given its electoral votes to the Democratic candidate in every election for the past 24 years, with no end in sight as its

Democratic majority grows larger in each election. Since most states use a "winner takes all" electoral system, individual voters in these "pre-determined" states believe that their votes makes no difference, regardless of which party they belong to. Even if the election appears close nationwide, voters perceive that their vote is "wasted" because the outcome of their state is virtually certain. Only in the "swing states," the handful of states with no strong leaning toward either party, do voters feel their vote could make a difference.

ILLEGITIMACY

Two aspects of the Electoral College create the possibility of a perceived "illegitimate president." Most obvious is the scenario in which the winner of popular vote loses the Electoral College vote and thus does not become the president, an outcome that has occurred more than once in American history. Most recent was the 2000 election, in which Al Gore lost the electoral vote (after a protracted legal battle) despite beating George W. Bush in the popular vote by more than 500,000 votes nationwide. This was the fourth (or fifth) time in our nation's history that an inconsistency between the electoral and popular votes had occurred, the others being 1824, 1876, and 1888 (and 1960, some argue). While rare, the possibility in any given election that this outcome *could* occur adds to the nation's sense of cynicism about this process.

Another less well-known aspect of our presidential electoral system, however, is even more troubling. Known as a "contingent election," the Constitution declares that if no candidate for president receives a majority of electoral votes, the House of Representatives shall choose the president from among the three top vote-getters (and the Senate shall choose the vice president). That, in itself, should give most Americans pause—handing the selection of the president over to one of the houses of Congress would seem to violate the separation of powers doctrine that is at the heart of our system of government. But the manner of the House vote, as dictated by the Constitution, is even more inequitable than the allocation of electors discussed earlier.

The framers of the Constitution, in a political concession to the smaller states, granted a single vote to each state's House delegation. Thus, in a contingent election decided by the House, the 584,000 residents of Wyoming, the 626,000 residents of Vermont, the 737,000 residents of Alaska and the 739,000 residents of North Dakota would have an equal say in electing the president as the 39 million residents of California, the 26 million residents of Texas, the 19 million residents of Florida and the 19 million residents of New York.

But that's not all. Not only is the contingent election grossly inequitable, it also lacks any accountability. The citizens of each state have no direct control over their state's vote. The members of each state's House delegation have total latitude to vote as they wish. For the seven states with just one Representative—Alaska, Delaware, Montana, North Dakota, South Dakota, Vermont, and Wyoming—one single individual would decide how his or her state's vote for president should be cast. Adding to the lack of accountability is the fact that rules adopted by the House of Representatives in 1825 stipulated that the voting within each states' delegations be done in secret. Except in the case of the seven states with just one representative, the public would have no way of knowing how their individual representatives voted.

Even worse is what happens if a state's delegation is split evenly between Democrats and Republicans voting along party lines. The Constitution gives no guidance for such a case, stating simply that "in choosing the President, the votes shall be taken by states, the representation from each state having one vote." But the 1825 House of Representative rules *do* address that situation, and they say that if a delegation is divided, it shall have no vote. By way of example, let's consider how that would have played out if the most recent presidential election (2012) had ended up in the House of Representatives. Three states—Iowa, Nevada and New Jersey—had House delegations that were equally divided between the two major parties. Assuming that those states' House delegations would have deadlocked, those states would have forfeited any say in the selection of the president.

The Constitution also dictates that if no candidate for vice-president receives a majority of electoral votes, the Senate votes to choose the vice-president. Since each state has two Senators, regardless of population, the same inequity exists as in the House vote: the smallest states get just as much say as the largest. What's more, because the Constitution stipulates that when the Senate is deadlocked the vice-president casts the tie-breaking vote, an absurd (and troubling) situation could result. A sitting vice-president running for re-election could cast the deciding vote on whether to grant him or herself four more years in office.

These are not merely hypothetical musings. Congress has selected the president twice already. The first time occurred following the election of 1800 when the electoral vote was tied, and the House narrowly selected Thomas Jefferson over John Adams. The second time followed the election of 1824 in which none of the four candidates running received enough electoral votes for a majority.

The 1824 election is particularly disturbing because the House selected John Quincy Adams despite his having received neither the most electoral votes nor the most popular votes. His 84 electoral votes were well below the 99 received by Andrew

Jackson, just as his 113,000 popular votes were well below Jackson's 151,000. But Jackson's 99 electoral votes fell short of the 131 needed for a majority, due to 78 electoral votes going to two other candidates: William H. Crawford and Henry Clay. Thus, the election was thrown to the House of Representatives which voted Adams into office. It did not matter that he had come in second, counted by either electoral votes or popular votes; each state's delegation was free to cast its single vote for whichever of the top three candidates it wished and a majority of delegations chose Adams.

Could this happen again? Without a doubt, in at least two possible ways. The first way would be an evenly tied electoral vote. The 2000 election came close, with a 271-266 electoral result (with one elector abstaining). With just a few shifts in electors, the vote could have been 269-269.

The second way would be if a third-party or independent candidate were to win enough electoral votes to deny either of the major-party candidates a majority, similar to what happened in 1824 with four candidates each receiving a number of electoral votes. With a growing number of Americans today identifying as independents, rather than members of either party—and the increasing disaffection with "politics as usual"—a viable third-party candidate might appear in the near future. According to recent polls, more Americans today consider themselves independents than at nearly any time since the late 1930s. In fact, more Americans today identify as independents (42 percent) than as members of either the Democratic Party (29 percent) or the Republican Party (26 percent). If trends since the year 2000 continue, within 15 years independents will outnumber Democrats and Republicans *combined*. According to a 2014 poll, that's already true for millennials (age 18 – 33). In a race with three—or more—

competitive candidates, the likelihood of Congress choosing the president and vice president becomes increasingly likely.

DIVISIVENESS

Even when the Electoral College "works"—i.e., the popular vote winner also wins the Electoral College vote—it fosters divisiveness among Americans. This should be no surprise. Divisiveness was built into its design, since its purpose was to maintain the sovereignty of the states. But two hundred years later, now that we are truly one nation rather than a confederation of independent nation-states, the Electoral College has not only outlived its usefulness, it is holding America back.

The winner-take-all awarding of electoral votes in the states is responsible for the notion of "red states" versus "blue states" that feeds today's hyper-partisanship. But the red-state/blue-state depiction is a distortion; not only does the country contain a diverse mix of political viewpoints, so do individual states. Even some of the states that are most partisan in their voting for president, will at the same time vote in the other direction for their members of Congress or state government leaders. Take Wyoming, once again, as an example. The last time a Democratic candidate for president won the state was 1964; for last 12 elections, the state has gone Republican for the president. Yet, over the same period, Wyoming voters actually elected Democrats to the governorship more often than they did Republicans, with the Governor's office held by Democrats for 28 years during that time, whereas Republican governors have held the office for only 24 years.

What's more, the depiction of America as a divided red-blue country ignores the largest single category of voters: those so fed up with politics they don't vote at all. In the last three presidential elections, the number of eligible voters staying home exceeded the number of votes cast for *either* of the two major party candidates. If election-night maps included those non-voters, most of the states would be depicted as neither red nor blue, but instead as white, depicting the winner as "none of the above." Depicting the country as red-versus-blue fosters state-versus-state divisiveness, and it leaves nearly half of the population within nearly every state feeling like "foreigners" in their own homes.

POLICY DISTORTIONS

Most troubling of all is the potential for the Electoral College to distort national policymaking. The candidates and their strategists are keenly aware that winning the White House depends on winning the "swing states"—those few states in which the popular vote is expected to be close—and they cannot help but be influenced by the particular political dynamics in those states. Today's technology has made this situation even worse. Through sophisticated use of polling, data analysis, and focus groups, campaigns now develop detailed analyses down to the level of individual voters and can tailor their campaigns to a handful of swing voters in the swing states.

Analysis of past campaigns demonstrates the undue attention presidential candidates pay to the swing states. In *The Empirical Implications of Electoral College Reform,* authors Darshan J. Goux and David A. Hopkins analyzed the number of public appearances by candidates George W. Bush and John Kerry during the 2004 presidential campaigns. The battleground states of Ohio, Iowa, and Pennsylvania topped the list with 45, 31, and 30 public appearances respectively, while the three largest U.S. states—California, Texas, and New York—were not deemed worthy of even a single public appearance by either of the candidates, despite the fact that together they held over one quarter of the entire U.S. population!

Or look at television advertising. A *Washington Post* study of the 2012 campaigns showed that out of the $800 million spent on television advertising by the two major-party presidential candidates, $669 million was spent in just five battleground states: Ohio, Virginia, North Carolina, Florida, and Colorado. And how much was spent in California, Texas and New York combined? Less than $250,000.

But does a campaign's focus on the swing states actually influence a candidate's policymaking? Susan Page of *USA Today* believes it does. In 2004, she wrote: "In recent weeks, [President Bush] has made a series of decisions boosting him in states that could be critical to his re-election. Last month, he announced that the federal government would buy back $235 million in offshore oil and gas drilling leases in Florida. He signed a 10-year, $190 billion farm bill popular in Iowa, Missouri and elsewhere in the Farm Belt. And he imposed tariffs of up to 30 percent on imported steel, an important issue in West Virginia and Pennsylvania."

Page goes on to describe how some of these decisions even went against president's own stated positions. She cites the Florida decision which would stop oil and gas drilling off the coast of that all-important battleground state, at the same time that the administration was forcefully pushing drilling off the coast of Alaska, considered a sure win for the president, and off of California, considered a sure win for John Kerry.

This quest for votes, at the expense of sound policymaking even irked some of Bush's own supporters. In the same *USA Today* article, Page quotes Steve Moore, president of the conservative *Club for Growth*, criticizing Bush for approving protectionist measures: "One week he's the president of Pennsylvania, and the next week he's the president of Iowa."

Even some prominent politicians openly acknowledge this pandering. Consider the statement by Pennsylvania's then-senior senator, Republican Arlen Specter, in 2011, when his state was considering adopting the more equitable approach of allocating electoral votes by congressional district, rather than statewide. Specter opposed the move specifically because it would threaten the benefits of being a battleground state, saying "I think it'd be very bad for Pennsylvania because we wouldn't attract attention from Washington on important funding projects for the state. It's undesirable to change the system so presidents won't be asking us always for what we need, what they can do for us."

NEVER AGAIN REPEATED

Perhaps the most compelling argument against the Electoral College is its failure to ever be copied. In the more than two centuries since our nation's founding, democracy has spread throughout the world, yet not a single country has chosen to elect its chief executive using our system. Nor has a single U.S. state used this approach to elect its governor. And it's not due to a lack of opportunities: since the late 1700s, most states have fully revamped their constitutions three, four or even five times. There have been over 230 state Constitutional Conventions. Yet not a single state has modeled its electoral process after the Electoral College. Every state elects its governor by direct popular vote. Can you imagine the outcry if a politician were to argue that some voters in their state should have a greater say about who will be governor than other voters, just because of where they live?

WERE THE FOUNDERS CRAZY?

Defenders of the Electoral College often base their arguments on the notion that it represents the wisdom of the constitutional framers, yet ironically those who drafted the Constitution were less enamored of their work than many Americans today, who hold in reverence every word and punctuation mark therein. For four months, the delegates to the Constitutional Convention debated and argued over nearly every detail, and in the end, none of them was entirely pleased with the results. Some delegates walked out of the convention; of the 55 delegates in attendance over the four months, only 39 signed the document. There was dissent even before the convention started. Rhode Island refused to send any delegates at all, opposing the convention's very premise that a stronger central government was needed. Patrick Henry, famous for his cry of "Give me liberty or give me death," refused to participate despite his appointment as a Virginia delegate, reputedly saying he "smelled the rat" of "a new monarchy."

As the framers constructed the Constitution, each section was put to a vote. Of the nearly one hundred votes taken on the various sections, only a handful passed unanimously. Compromises were made on nearly every issue: the structure of the Congress, how members of the Congress would be elected, the powers of the president, how the president would be elected, whether there should even be a single president. Each of these decisions, and more, were fiercely debated. On multiple occasions, the delegates changed their minds, voting for new language that directly contradicted what had been passed earlier.

And of all of the issues considered, those surrounding the nation's chief executive were the most fiercely contested. Even the notion of a single chief executive, something we take for granted today, was not a foregone conclusion (I discuss this in more detail in Chapter Eleven). But as much as the framers wrestled with the form of the executive branch—a single president, a council, or both—they wrestled even more with the method of selection.

It is often said that the framers rejected a popular vote for the president because of their distrust of "the people." But in fact, there were many reasons why a presidential popular vote, when proposed at the Constitutional Convention, failed to win support. It is true that some delegates considered a popular vote to be "too much democracy." Others however, feared just the opposite: that a national popular vote might lead the nation back toward monarchy, with the public susceptible to charismatic, but potentially despotic, candidates. For other delegates, more practical concerns held sway. They questioned the practicality of a national election, given the size of the country and its limited transportation and communications networks. There were no national or even state newspapers, the telegraph was many decades in the future, and travel within and between the former colonies was slow and often treacherous. George Washington barely made it home alive after the Constitutional Convention, his carriage nearly crashing into a flood-laden stream when a rotted bridge collapsed under his horses.

Further complicating the matter were the political tensions surrounding the diversity of voting rights among the states. Some states granted voting rights only to those with a certain amount of wealth or ownership of land, while others granted such rights more broadly. Some states granted free black citizens the right to vote; others did not. The convention had already nearly disbanded over the question of whether slave populations would be included in the count for determining representation in the Congress. The convention was saved only by the "3/5 compromise," with each slave counting as 3/5 of a person for such purposes, a concession to the slave-owning states to keep them from walking away. In the face of these political tensions, the delegates feared that trying to devise a national popular vote for president might end the convention for good.

Other approaches proposed as alternatives to a popular vote were also problematic. Selection of the president by the Congress was discussed at great length and for much of the four months of the convention was the preferred method. But there was concern that this would undermine the desired independence between the branches of government, by making the president beholden to the Congress. Selection of the president by the state legislatures was rejected because of a general distrust of these bodies by the delegates; the failure of the state governments to resolve growing conflicts among themselves had led to the call for the convention in the first place. Several delegates advocated for the governors of the thirteen states to select the president, but that proposal failed to gain much support. At one point it was even proposed that a small group of members of Congress—selected by lottery—should choose the president, on the idea that the uncertainty of which members of Congress would be involved would maintain the independence of the two branches.

Almost in desperation, as the delegates battled the clock, the Electoral College was devised as a complex set of compromises. It retained the sovereignty of the states by giving them the primary power of selection. But it tempered this power; rather than being wielded directly by the legislatures or governors of the states, it only gave the legislatures the right to appoint electors, whom the framers expected to act as free agents in their thinking. The apportioning of electors by the combined number of Senators and Representatives of each state gave the smaller states more voice than they would have had in a national popular vote, but not fully equal to that of the larger states. And the contingent power of selection was given to the House of Representatives—where, in fact, the framers thought most elections would be decided—but with each state getting an equal vote, again giving the smaller states disproportionate power. The system was far from perfect, but it was seen as the least of all possible evils. It may seem unnecessarily complex and undemocratic from where we sit now, but at the time it may have been the only politically viable solution.

In the end, the genius of the framers was their dedication to getting the Constitution *done*, even at the expense of getting it *perfect*. Not all the delegates were willing to sign the document, and some of them actively campaigned against its ratification in their respective states, but most acceded to the words of Benjamin Franklin, the elder statesman of the convention, who on the closing day said: "I confess there are several parts of this Constitution which I do not at present approve, but I am not sure I shall never approve them…thus I consent, Sir, to this Constitution because I expect no better, and because I am not sure that it is not the best."

REFORM EFFORTS

Beyond all we've discussed so far—the convoluted mechanics of the Electoral College, the problems it poses for our democracy, the reasons why the framers created such an odd compromise —one fact stands above all others:

The overwhelming majority of Americans today support a national popular vote for the president and they have for quite some time!

Polls consistently show strong support in all states—large and small, swing state and not—for a national popular vote for president. In a 2007 national poll, 72 percent of Americans said they support direct national election of the president. That sentiment is consistent across the nation, differing little, if at all, between the small states that are thought to benefit from the Electoral College and the large states thought to be disadvantaged by it. Once again, let's compare Wyoming, which gets the most electoral votes per resident of all the states (one electoral vote for every 195,000 residents), and California, which gets the least (one electoral vote for every 709,000 residents). Recent polls show the same percentage of residents favoring direct national election of the president in both states: 69 percent in each.

Interest in reforming the Electoral College is so high that many citizens and states have, in recent years, begun taking matters into their own hands by attempting to do end-runs around this archaic system. In 2004, Colorado attempted to switch to a "proportional representation" system, in which the candidates would receive electoral votes in proportion to the percentage of the popular vote they received. Pennsylvania made an attempt in 2011 to adopt the method used by Maine and Nebraska, in which a portion of the electoral votes is allocated according to the results in each congressional district. Both the Colorado and Pennsylvania efforts failed, but not because many voters didn't want change. The problem with state-by-state reform is simply that many people are reluctant to have their state take such a step on its own.

This chapter would not be complete without mentioning a clever, although perhaps ill-fated, effort to do an end-run around the Electoral College, called the "National Popular Vote Interstate Compact." Under this plan, individual states would pass legislation mandating that their electoral votes be given to the candidate who wins the national popular vote, regardless of whether that candidate wins the state's popular vote. The legislation explicitly states that this would only take effect when enough states have signed on to control the 270 or more electoral votes needed for a majority. Until then, the participating states would continue to follow their existing methods of awarding electoral votes.

The initiative began in 2007 and has now been adopted by legislatures in 11 states and the District of Columbia, representing a total of 165 electoral votes—61 percent of the 270 electoral votes needed for activation. While this is more than halfway to the goal, the states that have signed on are thought to be the easy ones. Getting to the 270 votes needed to put this plan into effect may be politically impractical. What's more, while this initiative may sound simple, it actually presents a number of potentially disastrous problems should it ever be activated.

First, the Interstate Compact might not be constitutional. Not because there is anything unconstitutional about a state choosing to award its electoral votes in accordance with the national popular vote; as discussed earlier, the Constitution allows each state to decide how to apportion its electoral votes. However, the Constitution also says that no state shall enter into "any agreement or Compact with another state" without the Congress's consent. And it is hard to imagine the Congress agreeing to this type of end-run around the Constitution.

Second, any state that joins the compact could just as easily leave it simply by passing legislation, leaving the whole system at the whim of state legislatures and their changing partisan makeup. The compact attempts to address this problem by stipulating that if any member state withdraws six months or less before the end of a president's term, the withdrawal will not be in effect for that election. But since the president's term ends on January 20, that means that states could withdraw up until July 20, little more than 3 months before the election. If enough states withdrew to bring the total number of participating states below the threshold of 270 electoral votes, the whole system would be rendered inoperable, possibly in the midst of the election season.

It's also not certain that this six month provision is legal. Compact proponents defend this provision under the "Contracts Clause" of the Constitution, which prohibits any state from passing a law that "[impairs] the Obligation of Contracts." However, there are a number of complex constitutional issues that might support an opposite view. Imagine a scenario in which a state legislature withdraws from the Compact a week before the election, triggering a lawsuit from other Compact members. How long would it take the Supreme Court to make a ruling? And do we really want another case, as in the year 2000, in which the Supreme Court, in essence, selects the president?

CHANGE COMES IN STAGES

Probably no other aspect of the Constitution has been so consistently despised by the American people, and yet not a single one of the more than 700 congressional proposals to reform or abolish the Electoral College over the past two centuries has achieved success. As we explored at the beginning of this book, Constitution change is a nearly impossible task. In the case of the Electoral College, the task has its own particular challenges.

For the Congress to pass an amendment abolishing the Electoral College, it would have to be willing to relinquish some of its own power—not a likely scenario. After all, Congress holds the final power of selection of the president and vice president in the event neither ticket receives a majority of electoral votes. While rare, it has happened twice in our nation's history, and Congress is aware it could happen again. Indeed, it became more likely in 1961, when the Twenty-Third Amendment gave the District of Columbia representation in the Electoral College, coincidentally creating an even number of electoral votes. Thus, for the past 15 presidential elections, the possibility of a tie vote in the Electoral College has been possible, which would throw the election to the Congress to decide. The 2000 election was decided by only 5 electoral votes out of 538; a tie would not have been surprising.

The irony is that if we are serious about fixing the ills of the Electoral College, we need to accept the political reality that we must do so without changing the Electoral College itself. At least not right away. Like the framers of the Constitution, who heeded the adage to "not let the perfect get in the way of the good" we should embrace compromise in the interest of progress. Change sometimes must come in stages, if it is to come at all.

Some readers might be put off by my proposal. After all, presidential campaigns are bitter feuds. Some readers might rebel against the idea of giving the "loser" any leadership role. I would ask those readers to consider several things. First, the real power of this pledge is how it would transform the presidential campaigns; the need to carry it out would likely occur rarely, given that there have only been four elections in our nation's history in which the winner of the popular vote lost in the Electoral College. But the incentives that this pledge creates to win both the Electoral College and the popular vote would transform how candidates behave *in every election cycle*. They would be more focused on the issues that matter to all Americans, as opposed to just the swing state voters. They would travel throughout the entire country, rather than spending most of their time in the swing states. They might even be more civil to each other, with the possibility of having to work together hanging over their heads. I believe those are things that nearly all Americans would like to see happen.

Second, the person who wins the Electoral College would hold the actual presidency. While they would offer their opponent a role in their administration if they lost the popular vote, they would always be able to fire that person, just as they can with any other member of their administration. (But they might find that, to their surprise, having someone with a different perspective in their administration actually makes for better decision-making overall).

Third, consider how this would work when *your* preferred candidate is the one who loses the Electoral College despite winning the popular vote. Wouldn't you want to see him or her playing a role in leading the nation? I believe that, in the long run, our nation will be better served by bringing more fairness to our presidential elections than it will be by continuing the current divisive and inequitable system.

So because we cannot look to the Congress to fix the Electoral College, we should look to the presidential candidates themselves. And that brings us back to this chapter's pledge for the candidates: *"If I should win the Electoral College, but lose the popular vote, I will offer my opponent a role in my administration."*

We need not expect the candidates to make this pledge solely out of a sense of honor. This promise, it should be pointed out, would be a powerful campaign tool. A candidate making this pledge would demonstrate the courage and integrity that the American people seek in a president. That candidate would gain respect from the voters.

I acknowledge that this is less than a complete fix of the Electoral College. But it is far from insignificant. *It would be the first time in our nation's history that a national popular vote counted for anything.* That fact is startling. In our nation's 240 year history, we have never taken any action, nor made any decision, based on a simple majority vote of all Americans. Starting down that road would have powerful symbolic value. Let us call upon the presidential candidates to lead the way.

11

FORMER PRESIDENTS, AMERICA'S FUTURE

A PRESIDENTIAL ACT OF WISDOM: For the president to enlist the nation's former presidents as a bipartisan council in ongoing service to the nation.

> Personally, I wish we could find ways and means of making greater use of the services of former Presidents. They have a type of experience and knowledge that can be gained by no other men.
> —*Lyndon B. Johnson, 1957*

The presidency has become too much for one person to handle. Consider how much our nation has changed since George Washington served as our first president over 200 years ago: the size of the country is now 4 times greater, our population is nearly 100 times greater, our national economy is 3,000 times greater, and the federal budget is 400,000 times greater! Consider also the social, technological and economic complexity of today's political challenges, the dizzying pace of national and world events, and the overwhelming flow of information in today's digital world. The demands of today's presidency would push nearly anyone beyond the breaking point.

At the same time, the window of opportunity for the president to effect change has shrunk, as campaigning consumes an increasing share of presidential time. That and the increased polarization of our politics have inhibited the president's ability to focus on the long-term needs of the nation, at a time when issues such as homeland security, the economy, foreign policy, and immigration call for just such a perspective.

And not only must the president provide a long-term vision for the country and develop the policies to advance that vision, he or she must manage the world's largest organizational enterprise. The federal budget, now approaching $4 trillion, exceeds that of any other government or corporation in the world, and the U.S. federal workforce, with over four million employees and enlisted personnel, is larger than that of any corporation, and on par with any of the world's largest governmental workforces. The result of these demands is an office that cannot help but push the capacities of any one person near the breaking point.

Admittedly, today's presidents are not without help, surrounded by legions of aides, advisors, and analysts who are ostensibly there to help the president navigate the complicated waters of policymaking. Yet these staffers, with agendas of their own—and themselves subject to political pressures and short-sighted perspectives—may fail to provide the honest independent counsel a president needs. Let's be realistic: when you report to one of the most powerful individuals on the planet, you may be reluctant to offer opposing points of view. The result is that White House environments have become increasingly prone to a distorted view of the outside world and increasingly susceptible to unwise actions.

We might consider the way that the business world has addressed the perils of vesting too much power in one person. All public corporations—and many private ones—have a board of directors to provide guidance and oversight to the chief executive officer. Yet our national government—larger than any corporation on earth—has no such thing. Who can the president turn to for high-level independent thinking? Certainly not the Cabinet; its members are far from independent, serving at the pleasure of the president. And not the Congress; it was designed by the founders to counterbalance, not support, the president.

The answer is the nation's former presidents. The job of President of the United States is like none other in the world. The president-elect can only guess at what lies ahead. No one can understand the job's challenges as well as those few individuals who have lived through them. And these elder statesmen, having already achieved the pinnacle of political success, with no higher office to pursue, are uniquely situated to work wholeheartedly for the long-term good of the nation, unfettered by the short-term expediencies of re-election strategies or party politics. Even, I would argue, should a former president have a personal tie to a sitting president, as is possible pending the outcome of the 2016 election.

A Fair Return On Our Investment

A bedrock principle of success in the business world is to "invest in your people." Most assuredly we invest in our presidents. Millions of taxpayer dollars are expended for the president's salary, Secret Service protection, Air Force One, operations and maintenance of the White House, and other expenses. In 2015, the White House staff totaled nearly 500, with an annual payroll of $40 million. And these staff are only part of the Executive Office of the president, which typically includes ten to fifteen entire agencies supporting the president's activities. Over 1,700 people worked for the Executive Office of the president in 2015, with an annual budget of more than $750 million. Millions more are spent, after the president leaves office, on the presidential pension, Secret Service protection, medical care, health insurance, and travel, office and staff expenses for the rest of the former president's life.

It wasn't always this way. For nearly 70 years after the signing of the Constitution, Congress provided no funds for presidential staff at all. In 1857, Congress broke with tradition and provided $2,500 so the president could hire one clerk. As recently as the 1930s, the presidential staff numbered fewer than 40.

Similarly, for almost 170 years, presidents received neither a pension nor other retirement benefits. It was only with the passage of the 1958 Former Presidents Act that these benefits were created. By 2000 the presidential retirement benefits mandated by that Act were costing the federal government $26 million per year. In addition, the federal government now spends nearly $90 million per year to maintain and staff the 13 Presidential Libraries, all of which have been created since Franklin Roosevelt established the tradition in 1939.

I am not arguing there is anything wrong with providing benefits to our former presidents. They have given much to our country. What *is* wrong, however, is our failure to take full advantage of the knowledge and expertise they have gained at considerable taxpayer expense. We can no longer afford to squander that investment. Our nation's challenges in the 21st century are too great.

PRECEDENTS

Tapping the skills, knowledge, and insight of former presidents for the good of the nation is a tradition that, in fact, goes back a long way. I am simply advocating for that tradition to be taken to a higher level. In their 2012 book, *The Presidents Club: Inside the World's*

Most Exclusive Fraternity, authors Nancy Gibbs and Michael Duffy chronicle the roles that former presidents have played since Harry Truman and Herbert Hoover lightheartedly gave the club its name. As Gibbs and Duffy describe:

> On January 20, 1953, at the inauguration of Dwight Eisenhower, Truman greeted Herbert Hoover on the platform. 'I think we ought to organize a former presidents club,' Hoover suggested. 'Fine,' Truman replied. 'You be the President of the club. And I will be the Secretary.'

Over the seven decades that followed, right up until today, former presidents have played key roles for the nation. This has not been entirely new; earlier presidents had consulted, at times, with their predecessors. In fact, George Washington himself, the first president, was called into service by John Adams, his successor to the office, to command the nation's military in 1798 as war with France was threatening.

In the post-World War II era, the trend accelerated. As former presidents lived longer, the federal government grew ever-larger, and the nation's challenges grew more complex, presidents increasingly engaged with their predecessors, sometimes privately, and sometimes quite publicly.

Even before the naming of "the club" in 1953, Democratic President Truman had utilized former Republican President Hoover's assistance to an unprecedented degree. When Truman invited Hoover to the White House in 1945 to discuss how America might shoulder the task of feeding a Europe devastated by the Second World War, the New York Times editorialized in support of "the two men who, working in concert, should be able to do more than any two men in America toward relieving the distress of 100,000,000 people." Later, Truman would enlist Hoover to convince a Republican Congress of the need for America to play a new role on the world stage as the Cold War unfolded. And Truman went so far as to place Hoover at the head of a commission to completely revamp the executive branch of the U.S. government, including the presidency itself.

While Truman's successor, Republican President Eisenhower, took a more "go it alone" approach, Democratic President John F. Kennedy, who followed Eisenhower, made good use of the club. First, the president's well-publicized consultation with Eisenhower after the failed attempted invasion of Cuba at the Bay of Pigs created a show of bipartisanship that strengthened the nation's confidence in the government during that difficult time. Then, as Kennedy faced one of the nation's most dire threats of the modern era—the installation of Soviet nuclear missiles in Cuba a mere two minutes flight time from the U.S. coast—Kennedy consulted every one of the living former presidents—Hoover, Truman, and Eisenhower—before taking action, going against the strong opinions of even his own advisors. Kennedy's intuition—supported by the former presidents—proved right. The Soviets backed down and withdrew the missiles.

Democrat Lyndon Johnson also relied heavily on Eisenhower throughout his presidency as he faced the challenges of the Vietnam War, a matter for which Eisenhower, former Supreme Allied Commander in Europe during World War II, could provide unparalleled advice. Richard Nixon, perhaps recognizing that these relationships should be an ongoing aspect of the presidency, created a post of "Special Assistant to the President for Liaison with Former Presidents," and had the government purchase a townhouse across from the White House for use by former presidents when visiting Washington. The townhouse is still used for that purpose today.

President Reagan was the first to use all living former presidents as a team when he asked former Presidents Nixon, Ford, and Carter to travel to Egypt to represent the U.S. at the funeral of slain Egyptian leader Anwar Sadat. Their gathering with Reagan before embarking was the first time in history that four presidents had been together at the White House. Nixon later carried out a unique mission for President Reagan, meeting privately with Russian Prime Minister Gorbachev and serving as a de facto emissary between the two world leaders.

President Clinton pioneered a different role for the former presidents when he asked former Presidents Bush, Ford, and Carter, as well as Nancy Reagan representing her husband, to join him in convening the 1997 *Presidents' Summit for America's Future.* The 3-day event, attended by nearly 30 governors, 100 mayors, 145 community delegations, and numerous prominent businesspeople, resulted in the creation of the *America's Promise Alliance,* now the nation's largest partnership dedicated to improving the lives of children and youth. The alliance now encompasses more than 400 partner organizations and in 2010 launched the *Grad Nation Campaign* with the goals of achieving a 90 percent high school graduation rate nationwide by 2020 and regaining America's standing as first in the world in college completion.

President George W. Bush, in a reprise of Truman's use of former President Hoover to address a humanitarian crisis, enlisted former Presidents Clinton and (George H.W.) Bush to raise hundreds of millions of dollars in relief funds after the 2004 Asian tsunami and the 2010 Haitian earthquake.

And following Election Day in 2008, then President-elect Obama suggested to President Bush that a gathering be held at the

White House with both of them and the three living former presidents as a show of national bipartisan unity. In early January of 2009, President Bush hosted that historic event, joined by Obama and former Presidents Carter, (George H.W.) Bush, and Clinton, featuring public remarks and celebratory photos, followed by a closed-door luncheon and discussion among the five former, current, and future presidents.

So we can see what former presidents can accomplish when they work for the good of the nation, both individually and jointly. But their ongoing service has been sporadic and entirely at the whim of the sitting president. It is time to turn the Presidents Club into a Former Presidents *Council*: a more focused, consistent and public demonstration of bipartisan leadership. We need these "elder statesmen" to send an ongoing message of national unity to counteract the divisiveness so rampant in our country today. America's ship of state needs all hands on deck.

A FOURTH BRANCH OF GOVERNMENT

Our government consists, of course, of three branches: the legislative, executive, and judicial. The Former Presidents Council could almost be considered a fourth branch, operating not with constitutionally-vested authority, but rather with moral authority. With some exceptions that I will describe later, the sitting president would decide what role to ask this council to perform and it would then fall to the council to decide whether to accept the request. Let me suggest four areas ripe for the council's leadership:

> *Collegial support, counsel, and encouragement to the sitting president.*
> At the Bush-Obama transition luncheon with the former presidents in 2009, President-elect Obama said: "All the gentlemen here understand the pressures and possibilities

of this office and for me to have the opportunity to get advice, good counsel, and fellowship with these individuals is extraordinary." All well and good. But why should this be extraordinary? These events should be a regular part of the presidency. A wise president might host such gatherings every three months for the "advice, good counsel, and fellowship" that only the former presidents can provide.

Humanitarian aid. The fundraising by George H.W. Bush and Bill Clinton for tsunami and earthquake relief was an inspirational demonstration of what two leaders from opposing parties—working together—can accomplish. The president could ask the Former Presidents Council to undertake one such humanitarian effort per year, either selected by the president, or jointly chosen by the former presidents.

Civic Leadership. Many domestic issues would benefit from a concerted effort by the former presidents, in the manner of the *Presidents' Summit for America's Future* described earlier. As with humanitarian aid, the president could select the issue or ask the former presidents to select one issue per year to which they would lend their collective support.

Diplomacy. A president—whether sitting or former—brings a sense of gravitas to diplomatic engagement with world leaders that no other American can match. Since the president cannot possibly respond to all the competing demands for his or her time, the former presidents have a unique ability to serve in his or her stead, when needed.

They already have relationships with many world leaders, sometimes stronger than the sitting president's. Former presidents have played this role before: the delegation of former presidents sent to Sadat's funeral, Clinton's deployment of Jimmy Carter to negotiate with North Korea's Kim Il Sung, Obama's enlistment of Clinton to secure the release of two American journalists from North Korea. Imagine all the former presidents working as a team to resolve the Israeli-Palestinian conflict. Or rallying international partners to support future U.S. diplomatic or military efforts that may arise. The Former Presidents Council could be a powerful "force multiplier" to meet America's 21st century geopolitical challenges.

These four functions of a Former Presidents Council—collegial support, humanitarian aid, civic leadership, and diplomacy—would provide a strong boost to the presidency and would send a powerful message of bipartisan leadership to the nation.

But let me suggest a more ambitious role for this council. It has been a tradition—albeit with exceptions—for former presidents to be silent about the actions of a sitting president. As individuals perhaps, that tradition should continue. But as a council of former presidents, there may be times to leave such silence in the past. If a situation is sufficiently grave and the council is united in its stance, and if they have consulted privately with the president to no effect, then it might be to the nation's benefit for them to speak out publicly. In the face of impulsive action by a sitting president, the council could serve as a voice of reason. When political tempers are flaring, the council could be a calming and unifying voice. And when the president and the Congress are stuck in gridlock, the council could provide the leadership needed to move past the impasse.

Where might we be now had former Presidents Ford, Carter, H.W. Bush and Clinton offered their bipartisan wisdom to the nation as we faced the difficult decisions following the 9/11 attacks? If these four elder statesmen—with their powerful collective experience—had chosen to speak out with a common voice, might they have been able to divert the president and Congress from the ill-fated decision to invade Iraq? Who, but these four men, could have exercised sufficient moral and persuasive authority to question that regrettable course of action?

Or consider the 2013 congressional budget stalemate that led to a 16-day shutdown of the government. Could the former presidents, as a team, have played a mediation's role to bring the president and Congress together to find a solution to the impasse?

Our country is facing many challenges that the president and Congress cannot seem to address: immigration, stagnating wages, the national debt, educational attainment, and more. What if the next president were to ask the five living former presidents— Jimmy Carter, George H.W. Bush, Bill Clinton, George W. Bush, and Barack Obama (soon to be in this role)—to bring their collective knowledge and hard-won experience to bear on these issues? Imagine the impact that a bipartisan proposal from these five would have. Presidential historian Doug Brinkley, commenting on the 2009 gathering of the former presidents at the White House, said: "If [President Obama] has a policy initiative that he wants to lead the country behind ... if he could get the signatures, the green light from all of the ex-presidents to say, 'Not only am I for this, but I have all of the ex-presidents backing me'—that's powerful."

The need for a council to play such a role was, in fact, considered quite seriously by the Founding Fathers. While today for granted the idea of a single president heading the executive branch, the framers of the Constitution considered several approaches to the executive branch: a single president, an executive council instead of a single president, and what they called a "privy council" of independently-appointed individuals to advise a single president. A number of the framers were strongly opposed to a single executive leader. Such concentration of power bore too close a resemblance to the monarchy that had cost the thirteen states much treasure, and many lives, to be free of. They feared what some say has now come to pass, a so-called "imperial presidency" with constantly-expanding power.

After much debate at the Constitutional Convention, the proposal for a single president won out. Some delegates had supported that approach from the start because they favored having a strong leader. Some had been put more at ease because the president was to be limited to a single term (and when that limitation was changed in the hectic closing days of the convention, it was overlooked by many of the delegates). And some were willing to accept the idea of a single president because it was assumed that George Washington, the hero of the Revolution and the presiding officer of the convention, would be the first in that role.

Even so, considerable uneasiness remained among some about vesting so much power in one individual. George Mason, a leading delegate from Virginia, stated that "in rejecting a Council to the president we were about to try an experiment on which the most despotic Governments had never ventured." None other than Ben Franklin, the most senior and perhaps most respected delegate to the convention, expressed the opinion that "a Council would not only be a check on a bad president but be a relief to a good one." Nonetheless, a proposal for an independently elected six-person executive council to advise the president was rejected, eight states to three. The seeds of today's dilemma were sown.

NO ONE IS PERFECT

While most Americans would welcome the bipartisan leadership that a Former Presidents Council would provide, some might balk at the idea of giving power to a former president. After all, rare is the president who leaves office as admired as he entered. Look at the four living former presidents of our time: two failed to win a second term of office (Jimmy Carter and George H.W. Bush), one left office with an approval rating lower than any president in the last 70 years (George W. Bush), and one (Bill Clinton) allowed his personal weaknesses to overpower his political strengths.

But while all these men may have their political blemishes, the presidency is a crucible of character like none other. No one passes through that fire without gaining a greater degree of wisdom, judgment and humility.

Jimmy Carter's presidency may have been lackluster, but he went on to set the modern era's standard for post-presidential service. Bill Clinton, since leaving office, has gone beyond mere redemption and become one of the world's most respected elder statesmen. George H.W. Bush's post-presidential partnership and genuine friendship with Clinton (particularly admirable given Bush's loss to Clinton in his bid for a second term) has shown the nation how former presidents can rise above partisanship.

Even Democrats might acknowledge that George W. Bush's second term exhibited a type of maturation that perhaps only the trials of the presidency can foster. His leadership battling malaria and AIDS in Africa won him the praise of some of his staunchest critics. His help brokering a peace agreement in the Sudanese civil war was considered landmark. And he made more centrist political appointments, such as Secretary of Defense Robert Gates, so highly regarded he was retained in that post by Barack Obama until retiring three years later (the only Secretary of Defense to ever serve two presidents of two different parties). Bush's strong bipartisan cooperation in the presidential transition to Barack Obama's administration showed the world how our democracy functions when at its best.

Are these men perfect? No, they have their flaws like the rest of us. But together they could provide the type of bipartisan leadership our country has been sorely lacking. By demonstrating cooperation across party lines, they could inspire the nation. Their joint powers of persuasion could move the Congress to action. And their support of the president could enhance the functioning of that office.

Most people are inspired by this vision of our former presidents rising above partisan politics. They understand how this could positively impact our national politics. Some, however, question giving power to those no longer in office. Others are concerned that former presidents might not act ethically, even wondering if former presidents could be "bought off" by special interests.

Let me respond to those concerns. First, regarding giving power to individuals out of office, it is important to note that the power of a Former Presidents Council would derive purely from moral authority. This would be an *informal* gathering of these leaders, acting as private citizens. They would have no formal power under the Constitution, U.S. laws, or rules of government. Neither the sitting president nor the Congress would be under any obligation to heed their advice.

Second, regarding the dangers of this council acting unethically, the Former Presidents Council would have inherent checks and balances by virtue of being a bipartisan body. If a time were to arrive when all living former presidents belonged to a single party, then this idea would need re-consideration. But that circumstance has not happened for more than 30 years, and given today's longer life expectancies, is increasingly unlikely in the future.

Third, regarding the possibility the council could be "bought off," former presidents in this era have few concerns about money. While in office, they receive an annual salary of $400,000 with nearly all living expenses paid. After leaving office they benefit from a generous pension and, perhaps more importantly, the ability to earn large sums through speaking fees, book deals, and consulting activities. All of today's current and former presidents are multi-millionaires, with net worth ranging from $7 million for Barack Obama and Jimmy Carter to $70 million for Bill Clinton, and the others somewhere in between.

Indeed, concerns about our presidents' susceptibility to the influence of money are more appropriately placed on the time they are *in* office, or running for election, not after they leave. Given the billion dollars or more needed to win the presidency today, it is naïve to think that candidates and office-holders are immune from what some call the "structural corruption" such a system engenders. Indeed, it is only *after* they leave office that they have the financial freedom to truly act for the good of the nation, rather than for more narrow partisan interests.

TAKING THE FIRST STEP

So let us call upon our former presidents to repay the enormous investments we have made in them. Can we predict exactly how a Former Presidents Council would work in practice? Certainly not.

But neither did the founders know how the system of government they designed would work. It is time that America breaks out of doing things the same old way, and returns to experimentation with democracy. As we quickly approach the start of a new presidency, five individuals—Jimmy Carter, George H.W. Bush, Bill Clinton, George W. Bush, and Barack Obama—will have the power to transform American politics by coming together as a Former Presidents Council, and the next president can demonstrate true leadership by accepting their help.

How to get started? It's simple. Not only should outgoing President Obama host the president-elect and the former presidents at the White House for a luncheon, as George W. Bush did in 2009, but afterward they should all head to the presidential compound at Camp David for a weekend retreat. This would give them more time for the "advice, good counsel, and fellowship" that President Obama so appreciated at the 2009 luncheon, and allow them to go deeper into discussing the challenges the incoming president will face. It would be an opportunity for them to discuss the idea of a Former Presidents Council and how such as council might best support the new president. And the weekend retreat could set the stage for similar Camp David gatherings hosted by the new president with leaders and members of Congress. Those retreats are described in the chapter that comes next.

12

LEADERSHIP IS A TEAM SPORT: BROKERING PEACE IN WASHINGTON

A PRESIDENTIAL ACT OF LEADERSHIP: For the president to "broker peace" with Congress's divided political parties, so they can all work together for the good of the nation.

Presidents enter office with a handicap—a glaring gap between what the public expects them to accomplish and the (limited) tools at their disposal to meet those expectations. So a president needs to take a team approach and build strong alliances—even with those holding differing views—if he or she is going to fulfill the promise of the position.

The American people have come to see the president as the "chief policymaker" of the United States, setting the legislative agenda for the direction of the country. And presidential candidates have little choice but to go along with those expectations, trumpeting the legislation they will pass if elected. Yet the Constitution grants the president very little power in that regard (some might say *no* power). The primary role of the president, as conceived by the framers, is to execute the laws *created by the Congress*. Yet, perhaps because of the continual gridlock in

Congress, the public increasingly looks to the president to play a legislative leadership role.

As many of us might remember from school, the framers intended the federal government to have a "separation of powers." The Congress makes the laws, the president carries them out, and the judiciary interprets them and applies them to individual cases. The president's only power relating to the legislative process is the so-called "Recommendation Clause" which says the president shall: "from time to time give to the Congress Information of the State of the Union, and *recommend to their consideration such Measures as he shall judge necessary and expedient*" (italics added).

Unlike much of the Constitution, this clause is vague and fairly weak. A federal circuit court ruling in a case involving President Clinton in 1993 stated that "the Recommendation Clause is less an obligation than a right. The President has the undisputed authority to recommend legislation, but he need not exercise that authority with respect to any particular subject or, for that matter, any subject." An earlier ruling by the Supreme Court against actions taken by President Truman made the point even more strongly: "The power to recommend legislation, granted to the President, serves only to emphasize that it is his function to recommend and that it is the function of the Congress to legislate."

In fact, for well over the first century of the nation's history—until the early twentieth century—presidents mostly stayed out of Congress's way, rarely actively involving themselves in trying to influence legislation, except in emergencies or war. This more passive role of the president is mirrored by the history of the other part of the Recommendations Clause: what we now call the "State of the Union Address." Throughout the nineteenth and early twentieth centuries, no such address existed; the president provided the Congress what was called an "Annual Message"—a lengthy written report on the activities of the executive branch. This tradition was started by Thomas Jefferson in 1801 in reaction to Presidents Washington and Adams's decisions to address Congress in person; Jefferson rejected that practice, deeming it too "monarchical," reminiscent of the British royalty's annual "speech from the throne."

It wasn't until 1913 that a president dared break with the Jeffersonian tradition, when Woodrow Wilson—to the dismay of critics—revived the spoken address to Congress. But Wilson's decision to speak directly to Congress was more than just a change in style. It reflected a new view of the president as legislative activist, a role pioneered by President Theodore Roosevelt, serving from 1901 – 1909, who famously described the presidency as a "bully pulpit" from which to advocate a national agenda.

But Wilson had, in fact, been a proponent of an activist presidency long before Roosevelt took office, perhaps even influencing Roosevelt's embrace of that role. As early as 1886, Wilson, a political science scholar, had criticized the weakness of post-Civil War presidents and the Congressional domination of government in his PhD thesis *Congressional Government: A Study in American Politics* (which quickly became a classic of American political science). Wilson went so far as to suggest adopting the British parliamentary system—in which the prime minister leads both the government and the majority party—although by 1908 he concluded such a change was not needed, believing a president could use the power of oratory and a vigorous demeanor to assert leadership over the legislature.

While Theodore Roosevelt and Wilson may have set the stage for legislative leadership, the real breakthrough of the modern presidency came with Franklin D. Roosevelt's ambitious legislative agenda to take the country out of the Great Depression. With subsequent presidents emulating that role, and with radio and television amplifying the reach of the president's persona, the American people have come to take for granted the president's leading national role in passing legislation.

But because presidents have no real authority to carry out the role of "legislator-in-chief," they must exercise special skills to succeed. If a president can rally the American people around an issue, that helps put pressure on Congress to act. But that's easier said than done. Despite appearances on election night, few presidents enter office with a broad base of support among the American people. The typical winning presidential candidate enters office having received, on average, just 52 percent of the popular vote, barely one out of every two people voting. What's more, when we factor in that, on average, less than two-thirds of voting-age Americans actually cast a ballot, the typical winning presidential candidate has won the support of barely one out of every three voting-age Americans.

So just as important as rallying the American people, is the president's ability to rally the Congress into taking action. And to do that requires building relationships, especially in today's polarized political environment. In his 2010 book, *The Modern Presidency,* author James Pfiffner says that presidents are well-advised to "court" Congress, in order to "build up a reservoir of goodwill that can be called upon when needed in a close vote." He describes how "Presidents Truman through Ford used to invite members of Congress to the presidential yacht, the Sequoia, for dinner, drinks, socializing, and even (in Truman's case) poker games. These were not occasions for arm-twisting or lobbying for specific votes, but rather for low-key socializing and building up the rapport that might help in later situations."

But the Sequoia was decommissioned in the 1970s by President Carter as a spending cut, an act that was well-intentioned, yet perhaps "pennywise and pound foolish" for Carter himself, given how his strained relationship with Congress made for a difficult time advancing his agenda. And that was despite his own party holding majorities in both houses of Congress. Indeed, the Democratic majority in the House was one of the largest of the entire 20th century.

Ronald Reagan's presidency, following Carter's, was a different story. Despite Reagan's landslide win, he faced a Congress in which the Democrats held a strong majority in the House for all eight years of his presidency. And yet Reagan is considered one of the most effective presidents of the modern era. He and political rival House Speaker Tip O'Neill would famously put their differences aside when the workday was done, often sitting down together for drinks at the White House.

Reagan didn't limit his collegiality to Tip O'Neill. He engaged with other members of Congress, as well. Consider what House Ways and Means Committee chair Dan Rostenkowski, one of the leading Democrats of his day, said in a 2004 *US News and World Report* article:

> 'Hell,' Rosty recalls, 'Reagan used to have six or seven of us over to the White House just to tell jokes.' One time, he smiles, 'Reagan wore that plaid sports jacket, and he offered me Campari. I told him if he didn't have any gin, I would go out and buy some.' Then it was down to business. I told him, 'You and I can write some history,' recalls the chairman of the tax-writing committee. It was the beginning of tax reform. 'It's so sad now,' says Rosty. 'These people [in Washington] are so angry they don't even talk to each other.'

We need a president with the courage to reverse that trend. In fact, with the deeply fractious political environment in America today, we need a president who sees him or herself not just as a leader in the individualistic sense of the word, but as a "team leader," whose job is to listen to diverse perspectives, bring out the best in everyone, and help bring opposing viewpoints together. We need a leader who will broker peace between the two parties.

The political reform group *No Labels* has called for presidential candidates to "commit to meet with majority and minority party leaders in the House and Senate at least once a quarter... They can meet at the White House or on the Hill. Go golfing. Grab lunch. Just talk."

The *No Labels* proposal is a good idea—getting together for lunch or golfing would be a good start—but the problems in Washington call for much more. The president should be willing to meet with *any* member of Congress, not just congressional leadership. Consider the example of Abraham Lincoln, who was famous for holding "open office hours" during which any American could meet with him to discuss any matter, no matter how trifling. Certainly the president should be willing to do the same with the members of Congress; after all, they are all in Washington ostensibly for the same reason: to address America's challenges.

But the president should go farther: not just an open door policy, but actively reaching out to members of Congress on both sides of the aisle. Why not set aside Sunday afternoons for this purpose and each week invite a different group of Republican and Democratic members of Congress, and their families, to the White House? It would be a chance to get to know each other as real people and to discuss policy in a relaxed environment. The president's role would not be to try to persuade members of

Congress. Just the opposite: the president would be the "listener-in-chief," taking in all viewpoints. And if the president were not available, the vice president could serve in his or her place. In fact, the vice president could play a leading role in this overall effort at team-building and brokering peace.

While Sunday afternoons at the White House would begin to create a foundation of relationships, those gatherings could be just the start. The president could host retreats with members of Congress—leaders as well as rank and file—at Camp David, the presidential mountaintop retreat located just 60 miles from Washington. Why should one have to be a world leader to be invited to the presidential retreat compound? Jimmy Carter was able to broker a landmark peace deal between Israel and Egypt at Camp David in 1973. So why shouldn't the next president invite the warring leaders of *Congress* to Camp David to negotiate a peace accord for *Washington*?

President Obama actually tried to bring congressional leaders to Camp David several times in his presidency but, perhaps due to the timing of those efforts, was not able to make it happen. During his first two years in office, he barely reached out to Republican members of Congress, leaders and rank and file alike. It took him almost 20 months to meet one-on-one with House Minority Leader Mitch McConnell. The president himself acknowledged the shortcomings of his isolation, following the 2010 mid-term elections in which the Republicans took back control of the House of Representatives. It was after those elections, which Obama described as a "shellacking" for the Democrats, that he first floated the idea of a Camp David retreat with congressional leaders. Still, the idea languished until seven months later when, in the middle of a 2011 budget deadlock, the president once again floated the possibility. But in the midst of a political crisis, when tempers and passions are running high, there is an urgency that precludes the more measured pace such retreats require. John Boehner, Obama's rival as House Speaker declined, saying it was "not necessary," and even Nancy Pelosi, Obama's ostensible ally as House Minority Leader declined, saying a Camp David trip could delay progress being made at daily White House talks.

Following the 2012 elections, the Obama White House again tried to revive the idea. Authors Mark Halperin and John Heilemann write in their book *Double Down* that then-White House Chief of Staff Bill Daley "floated the Camp David plan — a weekend getaway for the congressional leadership and their spouses." But they say that "Michelle's East Wing staff shot it down: who wanted to be cooped up on a cold day in the woods with [Republican Senate Minority Leader] Mitch McConnell?" If true, such an attitude from staff is disappointing. Peacemaking is rarely fun or easy. It takes work and it takes courage.

So here is what a campaign of teamwork could look like for the first 100 days of 2017. In January, the president-elect, the outgoing president and all the former presidents could go to Camp David for a weekend retreat, as I described in Chapter Eleven. In February, the newly sworn-in president could invite the congressional leadership from both parties to a Camp David weekend—along with their families—to get to know one another and identify issues they can work on together. The former presidents might participate in this weekend, at least partially. In March, the president could invite a small group of "rank and file" members of congress from both parties for a similar Camp David weekend and then the president could begin the Sunday afternoon get-togethers at the White House.

What it comes down to is this: since the Congress makes the laws—not the president—the president's number one goal should be to help the Congress succeed. We need a president who will pursue the long-term goal of healing a fractured government. We need a president who will build a team that includes all viewpoints, not just those of his or her allies. Reaching out to members of Congress, meeting with them at White House Sunday afternoons, and holding Camp David retreats would do more than just build relationships between the president and Congress. It would also help members of Congress start building relationships *with each other*. It is time for a president with the patience and courage to recognize that leadership is a team sport, and that the president's job is to lead the team.

PART III

★★★

TAKING ACTION

13

WILD CARD

This chapter is a short and simple message to our nation's leaders:

The acts of courage in this book are just suggestions. If you don't like them, then come up with your own. Be creative. Be courageous.

Not sure? Then ask your constituents. Isn't that what public service is all about?

Are you waiting for someone else to go first? That's not what courage is about. This isn't very hard. Try something. If it doesn't work, try something else.

Who is willing to start a Congressional Courage Caucus? Congress has hundreds of caucuses, from the Pro-Life Caucus to the Pro-Choice Caucus; the Progressive Caucus to the Tea Party Caucus. There's an Algae Caucus, a Friends of Lichtenstein Caucus, a Rodeo Caucus, a Candy Caucus and a Rock and Roll Caucus. Surely there's a need for a Congressional Courage Caucus.

The bottom line is this: if you take seriously the oath of office to support and defend the Constitution, and you take seriously the Constitution's goal to "create a more perfect union," then surely you can find ways to help rebuild our democracy—one simple act of courage at a time.

14

THE REBIRTH OF AMERICAN DEMOCRACY

JULY 4, 2026—AMERICA'S 250TH BIRTHDAY

The American experiment in democracy is far from over. The founders' vision of a self-governing nation—one that safeguards individual rights *and* is dedicated to the common good—still shines as a beacon of hope for people around the world.

We must not remain mired, however, in an outdated version of this noble ideal, one ill-suited to the 21st century. We need to reinvent our government using the same spirit of innovation and ingenuity that has made our nation great in so many other ways. A smaller government? Perhaps. Smarter? Absolutely. More efficient and effective? Without a doubt.

July 4th, 2026—America's 250th birthday—lies just beyond the horizon, a mere 10 years away. Will we celebrate a reinvigorated democracy or mourn the continued erosion of America's security and prosperity and the decline of our global leadership? The founders would not even recognize the challenges we face today. Are we honoring their legacy by clinging stubbornly to their 18th century ideas, or are we paying them the ultimate disrespect?

The time has come for a new generation of leaders to step forward. Leaders with the vision to reinvent what it means to govern. Leaders with the courage to create a vibrant 21st century American democracy. What this new democracy will look like is yet to be determined. But one thing is certain: the path forward must be taken one step, one act of courage, one politician, at a time.

So let us make good use of the ten years leading up to this landmark American birthday. Let us embrace this call to action: for every single member of Congress, and the president of this great nation, to undertake at least one act to rebuild our democracy. And next year, let us call for them to undertake two acts. And then, three acts and so on. Step by step, year by year, we can rebuild our democracy.

Imagine the best minds of America competing to solve our problems. Imagine the president working in partnership with his or her predecessors, and reaching out in a spirit of teamwork to members of Congress. Imagine the presidential candidates pledging to respect the popular vote. Imagine members of Congress coming together on each other's turf, walking in the shoes of average Americans, standing beside our troops, rejecting the filibuster, earmarks, and ideological pledges, and bringing the best and brightest of their constituents—from across the political spectrum—onto their teams. And perhaps most importantly, imagine members of Congress pledging to "do or die"—to step down from their posts if they are unable to produce results that gain the public's approval.

If we can make that vision a reality, the rest will follow: shared prosperity, security of our homeland, paying down the national debt, energy independence, a well-educated citizenry, and healthy vibrant communities. We will greet July 4th, 2026 with anticipation, not dread; with eagerness for the future, not longing for the America that once was.

Our generation bears great responsibilities: to our children, who will inherit the American experiment in democracy as it enters the next 250 years; to the citizens of the world—both free and not—who, despite America's trials and tribulations, still look to us for leadership; and to our nation's founders, who bequeathed us this great democracy. We must let none of them down.

America can still be an exceptional nation—in the best sense of that term—but an exceptional nation requires exceptional leaders. And exceptional leadership requires courage. The flame of political courage may be flickering, but it still burns. Together we can breathe new life into that flame. Together we can bring forth a new generation of exceptional leaders. All we need is to move from oath to action.

15

What You Can Do

★ ★ ★

This book is the start of a campaign to bring courage back to Washington. If you want to help, here are some things to do:

Contact your current members of Congress and candidates for office. Let them know you want to see them undertake at least one simple act of courage. Suggest your favorites from this book or let them choose. Or suggest an idea of your own.

Write a letter to the editor of your local newspaper. Call for current officeholders and candidates to undertake simple acts of courage.

Submit your own ideas for simple acts of courage. The acts in this book are just a starting point. Go to www.fromoathtoaction.com to submit your ideas. The best ones will be featured on the website each month, with rewards for those who've submitted those ideas.

Run for office. Don't wait for our leaders to act; become a leader yourself by running for office on a platform of courage. You could run for local, state, or national office. America needs courageous leaders at all levels of government.

Let us know if you've taken action. The campaign for courage needs allies across the nation. We'd like to learn what works and what doesn't and provide support to those who need it.

Sign up for the "Simple Acts of Courage" newsletter. You'll get updates about new acts of courage, politicians who have pledged to acts of courage, and news about leaders who have carried out such acts.

A portion of the proceeds from this book will be used for efforts to encourage members of Congress and the president to perform at least one of the acts in the book, or an act of their own creation. Follow the campaign at www.fromoathtoaction.com and contact us at fromoathtoaction@gmail.com.

And lastly, the message of this book—that simple acts of courage can transform the way an institution works—is applicable to any organization, not just the U.S. Congress and the presidency. Corporations, non-profits, colleges, local or state governments and other organizations could all use the concepts in this book, adapted as appropriate. CEOs, managers, board members and staff can all undertake acts of courage to help an organization achieve its goals. The author is interested in hearing from, or about, organizations that have used methods like these or are interested in trying them. Contact him at fromoathtoaction@gmail.com.

APPENDIX

Over the course of more than two centuries, only three significant structural changes to our system of government have been made through Constitutional reform. These three amendments—the 12th amendment, dictating separate candidates for president and vice President; the 17th amendment, dictating that U.S. Senators be elected by popular vote; and the 22nd amendment, limiting Presidents to two terms of office—each came about through a unique set of circumstances. By examining these three amendments, we will see why such circumstances are rare indeed.

TWELFTH AMENDMENT—CORRECTING AN ERROR

The Twelfth Amendment, passed by the Congress little more than a decade after the ratification of the Constitution, came about because the elections of 1796 and 1800 made it clear that the framers had created an absolute mess of a system for electing the president and vice president. The system created by the framers had no separate candidates for these two offices. The electors—often chosen by the state legislatures rather than by popular vote at that time—were to "meet in their respective States, and vote by Ballot for two Persons." The candidate receiving the most votes would become president and the candidate with the next highest number of votes would become vice president.

The first two elections—in 1788 and 1792—went smoothly because George Washington ran essentially unopposed. The election of 1796 however, which saw John Adams competing against Thomas Jefferson, revealed a major flaw. With the rise of political parties—a development unforeseen by the framers—Adams, the Federalist Party candidate, won the presidency while

Jefferson, the Democratic-Republican Party candidate, received the next highest number of votes and was thus vice president. The acrimony between these two men during Adams's single term in office was intense. They held vastly different views about the role of the federal government. It was clear that the Constitution's ability to create a "split administration" was a problem.

That in itself was not enough to spur Constitutional change, but the next election, in 1800, exposed another flaw, also due to the emergence of political parties. This time, the tables were turned, and Jefferson defeated Adams handily. But because the Constitution called for each elector to "vote by Ballot for two persons" and because the electors had adopted the practice of voting the party line, every single Democratic-Republican Party elector cast one vote for Jefferson and one vote for his running mate, Aaron Burr. With Jefferson and Burr in a tie, a decision needed to be made as to which man would become the president and which the vice president.

The Constitution dictated that the House of Representatives would decide the matter. Each state's delegation in the House would cast a single vote with a majority needed to select a winner. But the Constitution dictated that it was not the newly elected House, dominated by Jefferson and Burr's Democratic-Republican Party, that would choose, but rather the "lame duck" Congress still in office, dominated by the Federalists.

And that created problems. Although it was common knowledge that Jefferson was the intended presidential candidate and Burr the vice-presidential, the Federalists had such antipathy toward Jefferson that many Federalist House members attempted to put Burr into the presidency. Some state delegations cast their single vote for Burr, while others voted for Jefferson, and several state delegations deadlocked over their decision. Thirty-five separate votes were taken and still no candidate managed to get the necessary majority. Only after Alexander Hamilton, a leading Federalist voice, convinced enough of his peers that Jefferson, as odious as he might be, was less so than Burr, did the House place Jefferson in the presidency with a majority vote.

It had now become clear that the electoral system devised by the framers did not work. As the 1804 election approached, the Democratic-Republican Party, incensed by its treatment at the hands of the Federalists in the 1800 election, was determined to prevent another fiasco. On December 9, 1803, with the Democratic-Republican Party holding well more than the two-thirds majority needed in both houses of Congress, the Twelfth Amendment was passed. It took little more than six months for the required three-quarters of the states to ratify the measure. But although the amendment may have fixed the most glaring problems by dictating separate candidates for president and vice president, the underlying structure of the Electoral College remained in place and has continued to be the most debated, and perhaps most detested, part of the Constitution to this day.

What made the circumstances surrounding the passage of the Twelfth Amendment so unique? First, the political leaders of the country at that time held no mythic veneration of the Founding Fathers like we do today; many of them *were* the Founding Fathers and they had no qualms about tinkering with the document they themselves had created. Twenty-three of the fifty-five framers of the Constitution went on to serve at least one term in Congress during the period in which the First through Twelfth Amendments were enacted and only two out of those twenty-three are known to have voted against any of those twelve amendments.

Second, America was in the throes of change in nearly all respects. In just sixteen years from the ratification of the

Constitution in 1788 to the enactment of the Twelfth Amendment in 1804, the country had expanded from thirteen states to seventeen, its population had grown from well under four million to over six million, and its citizens had gone, within their lifetimes, from subjects of the British King to participants in an untried experiment in self-rule. The Louisiana Purchase had just doubled the land area of the country and Lewis and Clark had just embarked on their epic journey of continental exploration. Constitutional reform was merely part of this changing national landscape.

Third, the Congress had entered what would turn out to be a unique period in American political history. From 1800 until 1825, the Democratic-Republicans held more than two-thirds of the seats in both the House of Representatives and the Senate nearly continually. Such circumstances would rarely be seen again; from 1825 until today, only 8 of those 191 years would see one party holding the two-thirds majority in both houses needed to pass a Constitutional amendment. In the absence of that party dominance, Constitutional reform faces significant barriers.

SEVENTEENTH AMENDMENT—GIVING THE PEOPLE A CHOICE

More than a century passed after the enactment of the Twelfth Amendment before another change to the structure of our government was made. Americans today take for granted the right to vote for members of Congress, but until the 1913 passage of the Seventeenth Amendment, that right only applied to elections for the House of Representatives, not U.S. Senators. As originally written in the Constitution and in force for over 120 years, each state's legislature, not the citizens, selected the state's two U.S. Senators.

From the earliest days of the republic, the populace had been frustrated by their limited rights to *directly* choose the leaders of the nation. The president and vice president were chosen by the members of the Electoral College, and until 1824 even those electors were often chosen by the state legislatures rather than by popular vote. The U.S. Senators were chosen by the state legislatures. And the Cabinet members and Supreme Court Justices were chosen by the president subject to Senate approval. A citizen of the United States could cast a ballot for only one federal official: their member of the House of Representatives.

By the early 1900s, the control of the state legislatures over the selection of U.S. Senators had inflamed the public even more than their inability to directly vote for the nation's president. While the Electoral College system was still opposed by many Americans, that system had operated smoothly since the passage of the Twelfth Amendment; electors nearly always voted for the intended candidates, and only one election, in 1824, had to be decided by the Congress. But the selection of U.S. Senators by state legislatures was another story. That system had become riddled with problems.

First, unlike the Presidential electors, who were pledged to vote for their party's ticket, state legislators typically made no commitments to a choice of a Senate candidate, leaving the voters feeling cut out of the process. Second, charges of corruption and political gamesmanship were rampant as the legislatures went about their selection of the Senators. Third, it was not unusual for legislatures to waste inordinate amounts of time battling over the selection of Senators, while neglecting the ongoing business of the state. And fourth, at times some states could not even reach a decision, particularly if the two houses of their legislature were controlled by different parties, resulting in the state going entirely unrepresented in the Senate.

In response to mounting public pressure, a number of states enacted reforms, such as holding "advisory" popular elections for Senatorial candidates, the results of which were intended to guide the state legislature in its selection process. Some states went even further by requiring state legislative candidates to declare whether or not they would abide by the results of those advisory elections. But such reforms failed to quell the public's discontent. By 1912, twenty-eight states had taken the drastic step of calling for a Constitutional Convention to address the issue and it was widely believed that four more states—enough to reach the two-thirds necessary to force the Congress to convene the convention—would soon join in. With the threat of a Constitutional Convention hanging over their heads, and the fear that such a convention could spin out of control, Congress took action and on May 13, 1913 passed the Seventeenth Amendment. Less than a year later, the requisite three-fourths of the states had ratified the amendment.

What made this situation so well-suited to Constitutional reform? First, just as with the breakdown of the Presidential electoral process preceding the Twelfth Amendment, major components of American democracy were failing to function: legislatures were tangled up in knots for weeks on end; allegations of corruption were rampant; and Senate seats were sitting vacant when states deadlocked over their selections.

Second, the fact that the problems were occurring at the state level, not the federal, was a critical factor. The pressure on state legislators to relinquish their control over the selection of U.S. Senators was immense. The state legislators could see that attempting to retain this power would come at a severe cost: continued disruption of their legislative duties, charges of corruption and political gamesmanship, and threats to their very ability to hold onto their seats.

Third, this was a unique period in U.S. history. Immigrants were pouring into the country from abroad, an exodus was occurring from the countryside into the cities, and the modern manufacturing age was dawning. A rebellion against the "party bosses" and "political machines" that dominated American politics gave rise to the Progressive Movement—championed by Democratic and Republican leaders alike—which championed the connecting of citizens directly with the political process. States throughout the nation were instituting government reforms: primaries to take control of elections away from party bosses and give it to regular citizens; initiative and referendum processes enabling citizens to directly pass laws or change their state constitutions; and recall procedures to enable citizens to remove officials from office.

At the federal level, after forty years without a single change to the Constitution, four amendments were passed by the Congress and ratified by the states within a span of just eleven years: the Sixteenth Amendment, giving the federal government the right to collect income taxes; the Seventeenth Amendment, mandating popular elections for U.S. Senators; the Eighteenth Amendment, enacting prohibition of alcohol; and the Nineteenth Amendment, guaranteeing women's right to vote.

So these three factors—breakdown of a democratic process (the senatorial selection process), public pressure on state legislatures to fix the problem, and a wave of reform sweeping the nation—were a unique set of circumstances coming together to force the Congress to take action. Such a convergence of circumstances occurs rarely.

TWENTY SECOND AMENDMENT—BACK TO THE FUTURE

The last of the three changes to the structure of our democracy was the Twenty Second Amendment, limiting the president to two full terms of office. In the history of the republic, no sitting president had sought more than two terms until Democrat Franklin Delano Roosevelt did so and succeeded in 1940, and again when he was elected to office for a fourth time in 1944. In response, the Republican Party, upon taking control of Congress in 1947 for the first time in fifteen years, wasted no time in passing the Twenty-Second Amendment, and ratification was achieved by 1951.

This amendment brought to a close an issue that had been the subject of debate among America's political leaders since the drafting of the Constitution. The framers had argued vehemently over whether to impose a term limit on the president, in order to ensure what they called "rotation" in the office of the presidency. Ultimately, those opposed to a term limit prevailed. The sentiment for rotation, however, remained strong and a tradition of stepping down after two terms was started by the nation's very first president, George Washington. It was adhered to by every president who followed for nearly 150 years.

If not for the outbreak of World War II, Roosevelt might never have sought a third term. But with Nazi Germany sweeping across Western Europe in 1940, Roosevelt felt that no other American could lead the nation through the perilous times ahead. With the American people still strongly behind the president who had lifted the nation out of the Great Depression, Roosevelt chose to break with tradition as the end of his second term approached. His popularity and America's unease about the war raging overseas overcame opposition to his emerging one-man dynasty.

But Roosevelt's victory at the polls came at a cost; even during the election of 1940, the Republican National Convention called for a constitutional amendment to enforce a two-term limit "to insure against the overthrow of our American system of government." Over the next three years, eight state legislatures passed resolutions calling for such a measure and public opinion polls at the time showed well over half of the electorate favoring the notion. Congress took no action on the issue while the nation was embroiled in war, but once the war ended, it acted swiftly. With the election in 1946 of Republican majorities in both houses of Congress, the Republican leadership made amending the Constitution a top priority. On the very first day of the newly-elected Congress's first session, the Speaker of the House introduced a Constitutional Amendment limiting a president to two terms of office.

The proposal passed with significantly more than the two-thirds support required in both houses of Congress. Not a single Republican Representative or Senator voted in opposition. The proposed amendment also gained support from a number of Southern Democratic members of Congress. It must be remembered that many of these southern Democrats had been born within a few decades of the Civil War, and some were even sons of Confederate soldiers. Their antipathy toward a Northern elitist such as Roosevelt holding the reins of power for so long, even though a member of their own party, should not be discounted as a contributing factor.

So rather than a desire to improve the functioning of our democracy, the passage of the Twenty Second Amendment may have been inspired instead by several forms of political self-interest. Republicans were exacting payback from the Democrats for their domination of the presidency. Southerners were exercising their longstanding antipathy toward Northern elites. And members of Congress on both sides of the aisle were driven to reclaim the political power that they perceived Roosevelt's unprecedented tenure had taken from the Congress as a whole. Lastly, purely personal self-interest may have come into play. Service in Congress has traditionally been a stepping stone to the presidency. When a single politician can dominate the presidency for unlimited terms, the members of Congress are shut out of the opportunity to attain that power. Even some members of Roosevelt's own party may have harbored some animosity toward him for frustrating their political ambitions.

NOTES
★ ★ ★

INTRODUCTION

Fareed Zakaria, *The Post-American World* (New York: W.W. Norton & Company, 2008).

THE IMPROBABILITY OF CONSTITUTIONAL REFORM

[Over 11,000 proposed amendments to the U.S. Constitution] https://www.archives.gov/open/dataset-amendments.html (accessed July 23, 2016).

[Purpose of the "Constitutional Convention"] Max Farrand, *The Framing of the Constitution of the United States* (New Haven: Yale University Press, 1913) https://archive.org/stream/framingofconstit00farruoft#page/8/mode/2up (accessed July 23, 2016).

David C. Hendrickson, *Peace Pact: The Lost World of the American Founding* (Lawrence: University Press of Kansas, 2003).

[Stage coach between New York and Philadelphia]: http://www.berks.pa-roots.com/library/Stagecoach.html (accessed July 23, 2016).

[Referring to one's state as one's "country"]: John K. Alexander, *Samuel Adams: America's Revolutionary Politician* (Ranham: Rowman & Littlefield Publishers, Inc., 2002).

Ray Raphael, *Mr. President: How and Why the Founders Created a Chief Executive* (New York: Alfred A. Knopf, 2012).

[Historical partisan makeup of Congress]: http://www.senate.gov/history/partydiv.htm (accessed July 23, 2016); http://history.house.gov/Institution/Party-Divisions/Party-Divisions/ (accessed July 23, 2016).

CHAPTER ONE: ACROSS THE GREAT DIVIDE

[Charles Rangel residency]: http://www.politico.com/arena/bio/rep_charles_rangel.html (accessed July 23, 2016).

[Denny Rehberg]: http://www.tobaccorights.com/ctr/advocacy/legislatordetail.aspx?Legis ID= RehbXDenXXXXXXXX (accessed July 23, 2016).

[Earl L. "Buddy" Carter]:http://buddycarter.house.gov/about/ (accessed July 23, 2016).

[Bennie Thompson]: http://benniethompson.house.gov/ (accessed July 23, 2016).

[Streetcars in Washington, DC]: John DeFerrari: *Capital Streetcars: Early Mass Transit in Washington, D.C.* (District of Columbia: The History Press, 2015)

[Impact of commercial jet service]: http://www.cnn.com/2013/01/25/politics/social-congress/ (accessed July 23, 2016).

[Congress's three day work week]: http://www.newyorker.com/magazine/2010/08/09/the-empty-chamber (accessed July 23, 2016).

[Gene Green]: http://blog.chron.com/txpotomac/2011/01/special-report-houston-area-house-members-office-spending/ (accessed July 23, 2016).

[Ted Poe]: http://www.chron.com/news/houston-texas/article/How-each-of-Houston-s-Congress-members-spends-1710140.php (accessed July 23, 2016).

[Denny Rehberg]: http://www.tobaccorights.com/ctr/advocacy/legislatordetail.aspx?LegisID= RehbXDen XXXXXXXX (accessed July 23, 2016).

[Mike Ross]: http://www.politico.com/arena/bio/rep_mike_ross.html (accessed July 23, 2016).

[Chuck Schumer]: https://www.schumer.senate.gov/about-chuck (accessed July 23, 2016).

[First commercial television broadcast]: https://www.paleycenter.org/p-70-tv-countdown-july-1-1941 (accessed July 23, 2016).

[Number of television sets in 1946 and 1950]: http://www.earlytelevision.org/us_tv_sets.html (accessed July 23, 2016).

[Number of television sets in 1954]: http://www.lib.niu.edu/1993/ihy930341.html (accessed July 23, 2016).

Charles Peters, *Washington Monthly*, April/May, 2010: http://washingtonmonthly.com/archives/ (accessed July 23, 2016).

Matt Viser, *Boston Globe*, May 28, 2013: https://www.bostonglobe.com/news/nation/2013/05/27/representative-returns-house-after-three-decades-and-finds-eroded-traditions/U49Txz7dENOFLu1crHD6pN/story.html (accessed July 23, 2016).

[Benishek-Clarke "Joint District Tour"]:
http://benishek.house.gov/press-release/congressmen-clarke-benishek-announce-%E2%80%98joint-district-tour%E2%80%99 (accessed July 23, 2016).

[Benishek-Clarke "Joint District tour"]:
http://www.dailypress.net/page/content.detail/id/533256/Democrats--Republicans-working-together-.html?nav=5003 (accessed July 23, 2016).

[Benishek quote]:
http://blogs.wsj.com/washwire/2011/09/08/freshmen-lawmakers-try-bipartisan-tour/ (accessed July 23, 2016).

[Clarke quote]: http://benishek.house.gov/press-release/congressmen-clarke-benishek-announce-%E2%80%98joint-district-tour%E2%80%99 (accessed July 23, 2016).

[Bennet and Gardner joint tour of Colorado]:
http://kunc.org/post/bipartisan-visit-noco-businesses-reveals-successes-challenges (accessed July 23, 2016).

[Bennet and Gardner joint tour of Colorado]:
http://coloradopeakpolitics.com/2011/06/14/roadtrippin-the-bipartisan-tour-and-brandon-shaffers-uphill-battle-to-defeat-cory-gardner/ (accessed July 23, 2016).

CHAPTER TWO: THE RED BADGE OF COURAGE

[Number of veterans in current Congress]: Jennifer E. Manning, *Membership of the 114th Congress: A Profile*, Congressional Research Service, July 1, 2016: http://www.fas.org/sgp/crs/misc/R43869.pdf (accessed July 23, 2016).

[Tulsi Gabbard quote]:
http://www.nytimes.com/2015/02/18/us/bringing-a-rare-perspective-to-authorizing-war.html (accessed July 23, 2016).

Stephen Crane, *The Red Badge of Courage* (New York: D. Appleton & Company, 1895).

[Representative Raul Grijalva quote]:
http://thecaucus.blogs.nytimes.com/2011/01/08/live-blog-representative-giffords-shot/ (accessed July 23, 2016).

[Numbers of veterans in past Congresses]: R. Eric Petersen, *Representatives and Senators: Trends in Member Characteristics Since 1945*, Congressional Research Service, February 17, 2012 https://www.fas.org/sgp/crs/misc/R42365.pdf (accessed July 23, 2016).

[Number of veterans in past three Congresses]: Jennifer E. Manning, *Membership of the 114th Congress: A Profile*, Congressional Research Service,

July 1, 2016: http://www.fas.org/sgp/crs/misc/R43869.pdf (accessed July 23, 2016).

[Number of veterans in US in 2000]:
https://www.census.gov/prod/2003pubs/c2kbr-22.pdf (accessed July 23, 2016).

[Number of veterans in US in 2010 and 2035 (projected)]:
http://www.va.gov/vetdata/docs/QuickFacts/Population_quickfacts.pdf (accessed July 23, 2016).

[Charles Rangel quote]:
http://thelede.blogs.nytimes.com/2006/11/20/to-rangel-with-the-draft/?_r=0 (accessed July 23, 2016).

[Historical percentage of population performing military service]: Pew Research Center, *Most Members of Congress have Little Direct Military Experience*, September 4, 2013, http://www.pewresearch.org/fact-tank/2013/09/04/members-of-congress-have-little-direct-military-experience/ (accessed July 23, 2016).

[80% of veterans lost to incumbents]:
http://www.veteransnewsnow.com/2014/11/07/numbers-veterans-in-senate/ (accessed July 23, 2016).

[Embedded reporters]: http://www.journalism.org/2006/10/26/the-vanishing-embedded-reporter-in-iraq/ (accessed July 23, 2016).

CHAPTER THREE: FIRST, WALK A MILE

[Millionaires in Congress]:
http://www.opensecrets.org/news/2014/01/millionaires-club-for-first-time-most-lawmakers-are-worth-1-million-plus/ (accessed July 23, 2016).

[Average net worth of members of Congress]: Center for Responsive Politics:http://www.opensecrets.org/pfds/overview.php?type=W&year=2014 (accessed July 23, 2016).

[Average household income of Americans]: DeNavas-Walt, Carmen and Bernadette D. Proctor, *Income and Poverty in the United States: 2014*, U.S. Census Bureau, 2015:
https://www.census.gov/content/dam/Census/library/publications/2015/demo/p60-252.pdf (accessed July 23, 2016).

[Congressional salaries]: Ida A. Brudnick, *Congressional Salaries and Allowances: In Brief*, Congressional Research Service, December 30, 2014:
http://www.senate.gov/CRSReports/crs-publish.cfm?pid=%270E%2C*PL%5B%3D%23P%20%20%0A (accessed July 23, 2016).

[Paul Ryan quote]: *New Yorker*, June 20, 2016:http://www.newyorker.com/magazine/2016/06/20/inside-the-gop-trump-dilemma (accessed July 23, 2016).

[Charlie Summers, 30 Jobs in 30 Days]:http://bangordailynews.com/2008/10/03/politics/charlie-summers-30-jobs-in-30-days-defines-iraq-veteranrsquos-campaign/ (accessed July 23, 2016).

[Food Stamp Challenge, Van Hollen quote]: http://foodstampchallenge.typepad.com/my_weblog/ (accessed July 23, 2016).

[Food Stamp Challenge, McGovern quote]: http://foodstampchallenge.typepad.com/my_weblog/congressman_jim _mcgovern/ (accessed July 23, 2016).

[Joe Walsh quote]:http://politicalticker.blogs.cnn.com/2011/01/04/freshman-rep-pledges-to-forgo-federal-health-insurance/ (accessed July 23, 2016).

[Mike Quigley]:http://www.nytimes.com/2010/04/16/us/politics/16cncwarre n.html;

https://quigley.house.gov/newsroom/undercover-congressman (accessed July 23, 2016).

[2014 Poverty rates]: DeNavas-Walt, Carmen and Bernadette D. Proctor, U.S. Census Bureau, Current Population Reports, P60-252, *Income and Poverty in the United States: 2014*, U.S. Government Printing Office, Washington, DC, 2015: https://www.census.gov/content/dam/Census/library/publications/20 15/demo/ p60-252.pdf (accessed July 23, 2016).

[Incarceration rates]: http://www.prb.org/Publications/Articles/2012/us-incarceration.aspx (accessed July 23, 2016).

[Crime Rates]: http://www.nytimes.com/books/first/c/currie-crime.html; http://www.nytimes.com/2008/04/23/world/americas/23iht23prison.1 2253738.html?pagewanted=all&_r=0 (accessed July 23, 2016).

CHAPTER FOUR: LEADERSHIP IS A TEAM SPORT: ASKING FOR HELP

Warren Bennis, Patricia Ward Biederman, *Organizing Genius: The Secrets of Creative Collaboration* (New York: Basic Books, 1998).

[John Shimkus: Veterans Advisory Committee]:https://shimkus.house.gov/media-center/press-releases/shimkus-invites-vets-to-learn-about-new-law (accessed July 25, 2016).

[Tim Griffin: Veterans Advisory Committee]:
http://www.arktimes.com/ArkansasBlog/archives/2012/02/23/tim-griffin-va-chair-say-little-on-vets-center (accessed July 25, 2016).

[Linda Sanchez, Veterans Advisory Council]:
https://lindasanchez.house.gov/media-center/press-releases/rep-s-nchez-kicks-veterans-advisory-council (accessed July 25, 2016).

[Steve Pearce, Veterans Advisory Council]:
http://pearce.house.gov/VAC (accessed July 25, 2016).

[Kathy Hochul, Veterans Advisory Council]:
https://votesmart.org/public-statement/651689/congresswoman-hochul-announces-veterans-advisory-council-at-veterans-town-hall-in-lancaster#.V5TZS9JRThk (accessed July 25, 2016).

[Chris Gibson, Energy Advisory Council]:
http://gibson.house.gov/news/documentsingle.aspx?DocumentID=228224 (accessed July 25, 2016).

[Chris Gibson, Watershed Advisory Council]:
http://gibson.house.gov/watershed/ (accessed July 25, 2016).

[Chris Gibson, Agriculture Advisory Council]:
http://gibson.house.gov/news/documentsingle.aspx?DocumentID=236966 (accessed July 25, 2016).

[Sam Johnson, most conservative member of Congress]:http://www.samjohnson.house.gov/Biography/ (accessed July 25, 2016).

[Sam Johnson Youth Advisory Council quote]:
http://samjohnson.house.gov/news/documentsingle.aspx?DocumentID=355555 (accessed July 25, 2016).

[Sam Johnson Youth Advisory Council]:
http://samjohnson.house.gov/constituentservices/congressionalyouthadvisorycouncil.htm (accessed July 25, 2016).

[Jared Polis, First openly gay parent in Congress]:
http://abcnews.go.com/blogs/politics/2011/09/house-democrat-jared-polis-becomes-first-openly-gay-parent-in-congress/ (accessed July 25, 2016).

[Jared Polis Youth Advisory Committee]:
http://polis.house.gov/studentscorner/youthadvisorycouncil.htm (accessed July 25, 2016).

[Dianne Feinstein quote]:
http://www.feinstein.senate.gov/public/index.cfm/press-releases?ID=8500b5d9-905b-0a1d-6d3b-28fac1447f7c (accessed July 25, 2016).

[Campaign for a Presidential Youth Council]:
http://www.presidentialyouthcouncil.org/ (accessed September 4, 2016)

[House Resolution supporting the creation of a Presidential Youth Council]: https://www.congress.gov/bill/114th-congress/house-joint-resolution/47/text (accessed September 4, 2016)

[Doris Kelley, letter to the editor from Marcy Hartleip]: http://wcfcourier.com/news/opinion/mailbag/candidate/paid-endorsement-letters-for-oct/article_962f7166-dba5-11df-9ec4-001cc4c002e0.html (accessed July 25, 2016).

CHAPTER FIVE: CROWD-LEGISLATING

[Alexander Hamilton quote, The Federalist Papers, Number 72]: http://avalon.law.yale.edu/18th_century/fed72.asp (accessed July 26, 2016).

[Much of the history of innovation contests is taken from *Selected Innovation Prizes And Reward Programs*, KEI Research Note 2008:1]:http://www.keionline.org/misc-docs/research_notes/kei_rn_2008_1.pdf (accessed July 26, 2016).

[Longitude Prize]:http://www.americanscientist.org/issues/pub/the-british-longitude-act-reconsidered/1 (accessed July 26, 2016).

[U.S.'s first automobile race]: http://www.encyclopedia.chicagohistory.org/pages/2380.html (accessed July 26, 2016).

[X-Prize]: http://ansari.xprize.org/teams (accessed July 26, 2016).

Don Tapscott and Anthony D. Williams *Wikinomics: How Mass Collaboration Changes Everything* (New York: Penguin Group, 2006)

[Microsoft BlueHat Prize to address computer security threats]: https://www.microsoft.com/ security/bluehatprize/contest.aspx (accessed July 26, 2016).

[GE healthymagination Cancer Challenge]:http://newsroom.gehealthcare.com/battling-breast-cancer-with-five-breakthrough-projects/ (accessed July 26, 2016).

[Innocentive]: https://www.innocentive.com/ (accessed July 26, 2016).

[Skild]: http://www.skild.com/ (accessed July 26, 2016).

[Google Project 10^100]:https://googleblog.blogspot.com/2010/09/10-million-for-project-10100-winners.html (accessed July 26, 2016).

[Pepsi Refresh Contest]:http://www.pepsico.com/live/pressrelease/The-Pepsi-Refresh-

Project-Awards-13-Million-to-Support-the-Publics-Favorite-Idea03222010 (accessed July 26, 2016).

[Bloomberg Mayors' Challenge]:
http://mayorschallenge.bloomberg.org/ (accessed July 26, 2016).

[FastFWD]: http://technical.ly/philly/2014/06/04/fastfwd-city-philadelphia-pilot/ (accessed September 3, 2016);
http://technical.ly/philly/2014/10/01/fastfwd-phillys-public-safety-accelerator-rethinks/ (accessed September 3, 2016)

[LA2050 Challenge]: http://maker.good.is/myla2050.html (accessed July 26, 2016).

[Participatory budgeting]: http://www.participatorybudgeting.org/ (accessed July 26, 2016).

[Participatory budgeting in Chicago]: http://www.pbchicago.org/ (accessed July 26, 2016).

[Participatory budgeting in New York City]:
http://labs.council.nyc/pb/ (accessed July 26, 2016).

[Participatory budgeting in Vallejo, California]:
http://www.ci.vallejo.ca.us/city_hall/departments___divisions/city_manager/participatory_budgeting/ (accessed July 26, 2016).

[U.S. infant mortality rate, Washington Post, September 29, 2014]:
https://www.washingtonpost.com/news/wonk/wp/2014/09/29/our-infant-mortality-rate-is-a-national-embarrassment/ (accessed July 26, 2016).

[Stuxnet virus]:
https://www.washingtonpost.com/world/national-security/stuxnet-was-work-of-us-and-israeli-experts-officials-say/2012/06/01/gJQAlnEy6U_story.html (accessed July 26, 2016).

[Expense allocations of members of Congress]: Ida A. Brudnick, *Congressional Salaries and Allowances: In Brief,* December 30, 2014, http://fas.org/sgp/crs/misc/RL30064.pdf (accessed July 26, 2016).

[U.S. and China Gross Domestic Product]:http://data.worldbank.org/indicator/NY.GDP.MKTP.CD (accessed July 26, 2016).

CHAPTER SIX: NO LYING

[Pledge against new taxes]:
http://www.atr.org/ (accessed August 25, 2016).

CHAPTER SEVEN: NO CHEATING

[Strom Thurmond record
filibuster]:http://www.businessinsider.com/longest-filibuster-in-history-
strom-thurmond-rand-paul-2013-3 (accessed August 25, 2016).

[Filibustering of Civil Rights
Act]:http://blog.constitutioncenter.org/2016/04/the-filibuster-that-
almost-killed-the-civil-rights-act/ (accessed August 25, 2016).

[History of filibuster in the U.S. Senate]:
http://www.senate.gov/artandhistory/history/common/briefing/Filibus
ter_Cloture.htm (accessed August 25, 2016).

[Growth in size of House of
Representatives]:http://history.house.gov/Congressional-
Overview/Profiles/1st/ (accessed August 25, 2016).

[1841 change to House
rules]:http://history.house.gov/HistoricalHighlight/Detail/35501
(accessed August 25, 2016).

[Growth in size of
Senate]:http://www.senate.gov/artandhistory/history/resources/pdf/ch
ronlist.pdf (accessed August 25, 2016).

[Etymology of the word "filibuster"]:
http://content.time.com/time/politics/article/0,8599,1933802,00.html
(accessed August 25, 2016).

[Use of filibusters through the early 1900s]:Ted G. Jelen, Mark J.
Rozell, Michael Shally-Jensen *American Political Culture: An Encyclopedia*
(ABC-CLIO, 2015)

[Woodrow Wilson quote]:
http://www.nytimes.com/roomfordebate/2013/12/18/the-history-and-
lessons-of-congressional-crises/wilson-the-senate-and-cloture (accessed
August 25, 2016).

[Historical partisan makeup of the Senate]:
http://www.senate.gov/history/partydiv.htm (accessed August 25,
2016).

CHAPTER EIGHT: NO STEALING

["Bridge to Nowhere" USA
Today]:http://usatoday30.usatoday.com/news/opinion/editorials/2005-
05-17-alaska-edit_x.htm (accessed August 25, 2016).

[The ferry from Ketchikan to Gravina Island carried an average of
1,114 passengers per day in 2007, including both walk-on passengers and
those in vehicles, according to the Borough of Ketchikan]:

http://www.borough.ketchikan.ak.us/Archive.aspx?AMID=36 (accessed August 25, 2016).

[The Brooklyn Bridge carries 124,000 vehicles per day, according to the NY City Department of Transportation]: http://www.nyc.gov/html/dot/html/infrastructure/bridges.shtml (accessed August 25, 2016).

[The Golden Gate Bridge carries approximately 109,000 vehicles per day, according to the Golden Gate Bridge Highway and Transportation District]:http://goldengatebridge.org/research/crossings_revenues.php (accessed August 25, 2016).

[Office of Management and Budget definition of earmarks]:https://earmarks.omb.gov/earmarks-public/ (accessed August 25, 2016).

[Earmarks defended as being only a small percentage of federal budget]:http://www.rollcall.com/news/the_congressional_earmark_ban_the_real_bridge_to_nowhere_commentary-235380-1.html (accessed August 25, 2016).

[Quote attributed to DeTouqeville or Tytler]: https://en.wikiquote.org/wiki/Alexis_de_Tocqueville (accessed August 25, 2016).

[McCain position against earmarks]: http://thecaucus.blogs.nytimes.com/2010/11/16/mccain-who-battled-earmarks-watches-others-ban-them/?_r=0 (accessed August 25, 2016).

[Feingold position against earmarks]: http://www.jsonline.com/news/opinion/40567012.html (accessed August 25, 2016).

[Bachman position against earmarks]: http://talkingpointsmemo.com/dc/anti-earmark-bachmann-open-to-earmark-redefinition-for-her-district (accessed August 25, 2016).

[Boehner position against earmarks]: http://www.washingtontimes.com/news/2015/oct/28/john-boehner-reshaped-house-speakership-with-earma/ (accessed August 25, 2016).

[McConnell $2.8 billion earmark in 2013]:http://thecaucus.blogs.nytimes.com/2013/10/17/after-cutting-a-deal-mcconnell-draws-criticism-from-all-sides/?ref=earmarks&_r=0 (accessed August 25, 2016).

[Moran $404 million 2014 appropriation]:http://www.moran.senate.gov/public/index.cfm/news-releases?ID=4b7a8e5c-6fb5-4155-8304-59c061f4e239 (accessed August 25, 2016).

[Landrieu $310 million 2014 appropriation]
:http://www.huffingtonpost.com/2014/01/15/omnibus-budget-earmarks_n_4603141.html (accessed August 25, 2016).

[Abrams   tank
spending]:http://www.huffingtonpost.com/2013/04/28/abrams-tank-congress-army_n_3173717.html (accessed August 25, 2016).

CHAPTER NINE: DO OR DIE

[Incumbent re-election rates]:
https://www.opensecrets.org/overview/reelect.php (accessed August 17, 2016).

[Incumbent losses in primaries]:
http://www.centerforpolitics.org/crystalball/articles/frc2010030401/?upm_export=print (accessed August 17, 2016).

[2008 Senate election results]:
http://www.cnn.com/ELECTION/2008/results/main.results/#S (accessed August 17, 2016).

[2008 Congressional general election results]:
http://clerk.house.gov/member_info/electionInfo/2008election.pdf (accessed August 17, 2016).

[Historical incumbent re-election rates]: David C. Huckabee, *Reelection Rates of Incumbents: 1790 – 1994*, Congressional Research Service (CRS), March 8, 1995, http://www.thirty-thousand.org/pages/QHA-08.htm (accessed August 17, 2016).

[John Dingell, Jr.]: Manning, Jennifer E., Membership of the 113th Congress: A Profile, Congressional Research Service, July 14, 2014 Mannihttp://www.senate.gov/CRSReports/crs-publish.cfm?pid=%260BL%2BR%5CC%3F%0A (accessed August 17, 2016).

[John Dingell, Jr.]:
https://web.archive.org/web/20080201160204/http://www.house.gov/dingell/bio.htm (accessed August 17, 2016).

[John Dingell, Sr.]:
http://history.house.gov/HistoricalHighlight/Detail/15032395644?ret=True (accessed August 17, 2016).

[Debbie Dingell]:
http://www.clickondetroit.com/news/politics/debbie-dingell-wins-husbands-house-seat (accessed August 17, 2016).

[Abraham Lincoln quote]: Luther Emerson Robinson, *Abraham Lincoln as a Man of Letters* (University of Michigan Library, January 1, 1918)

[1995 Supreme Court decision on term limits]:
http://www.nytimes.com/1995/05/23/us/high-court-blocks-term-limits-for-congress-in-a-5-4-decision.html?pagewanted=all (accessed August 17, 2016).

[Proposed amendment to impose term limits, H.J.Res. 73 (104th)]:
Contract with America bill:
https://www.govtrack.us/congress/votes/104-1995/h277 (accessed August 17, 2016).

[State term limits]: http:/www.usnews.com/opinion/articles/2015/01/16/states-show-term-limits-wouldnt-work-for-congress
https://scholarworks.iupui.edu/bitstream/handle/1805/3618/thesis%20october%203.pdf?sequence=7 (accessed August 17, 2016).

[Current statistics on at-large city councils]:
http://kcmayor.org/cms/wp-content/uploads/2013/06/Municipal-Form-of-Government-Trends-in-Structure.pdf (accessed August 17, 2016).

[At-large city councils]:http://www.nlc.org/build-skills-and-networks/resources/cities-101/city-officials/municipal-elections (accessed August 17, 2016).

[New York's "Forty Thieves"]: Ralph J. Caliendo, *New York City Mayors, Volume 1* (Xlibris Corporation, 2010)

[Chicago's "Gray Wolves"]:
http://www.encyclopedia.chicagohistory.org/pages/540.html (accessed August 17, 2016).

[Helen Chenoweth term limits pledge]:http://history.house.gov/People/Detail/10886 (accessed August 17, 2016).

[Sam Brownback term limits pledge]:
http://www.fstribune.com/story/1487471.html (accessed August 17, 2016).

[Steve Moak pledge]:
http://www.prweb.com/releases/2010_07/stevemoakpledge/prweb4277894.htm (accessed August 17, 2016).

[Emergence of primary elections]: http://aceproject.org/ace-en/topics/pc/pcz (accessed August 17, 2016).

[Sore Loser laws]: Michael S. Kang, *Sore Loser Laws and Democratic Contestation*, Emory University School of Law, 2011,
http://papers.ssrn.com/sol3/papers.cfm?abstract_id=1809970 (accessed August 17, 2016).

[Supreme Court Ballot Access Doctrine]:https://www.law.cornell.edu/background/ballot/supreme.htm (accessed August 17, 2016).

CHAPTER TEN: ONE PERSON, ONE VOTE, ONE NATION

[Attempts to reform the Electoral College]: Gary Bugh, *Electoral College Reform* (Burlington, VT: Ashgate Publishing Company, 2010)

[Bringing members of the opposing party into the Administration]: http://www.politifact.com/truth-o-meter/statements/2009/feb/10/barack-obama/Three-Republicans-Cabinet-Most/ (accessed August 18, 2016).

[Kennedy offer to Nixon]: Richard M. Nixon, *Six Crises* (New York: Doubleday & Company, Inc., 1962)

[Lincoln]: Doris Kearns Goodwin, *Team of Rivals: The Political Genius of Abraham Lincoln*, (New York: Simon & Schuster, 2005)

[Electoral college in the U.S. Constitution]: https://www.gpo.gov/fdsys/pkg/CDOC-110hdoc50/pdf/CDOC-110hdoc50.pdf (accessed August 18, 2016).

New York State Election Law, Article 12—Presidential Electors And Federal Elected Officers: http://www.elections.ny.gov/NYSBOE/download/law/2015NYElectio nLaw.pdf (accessed August 18, 2016).

[1992 Presidential election results]:http://www.fec.gov/pubrec/fe1992/federalelections92.pdf (accessed August 18, 2016).

[Historical California and Wyoming presidential election results]:http://www.archives.gov/federal-register/electoral-college/map/historic.html (accessed August 18, 2016).

[Conflicting popular and electoral college vote counts]: Gary Bugh, *Electoral College Reform* (Burlington, VT: Ashgate Publishing Company, 2010)

[1825 Rules of the House of Representatives concerning contingent elections]: *Election of the President and Vice President by Congress: Contingent Election*, Thomas H. Neale, Congressional Research Service, 1999 http://congressionalresearch.com/RL32695/document.php?study=Elec tion+of+the+President+and+Vice+President+by+Congress+Continge nt+Election (accessed August 18, 2016).

[1824 presidential election]: George C. Edwards III, *Why the Electoral College is Bad for America*, (New Haven: Yale University, 20110

[2000 presidential electoral votes]: http://www.fec.gov/pubrec/2000presgeresults.htm (accessed August 18, 2016).

[Trends in party affiliation since the 1930s]: http://www.people-press.org/2015/04/07/a-deep-dive-into-party-affiliation/ (accessed August 18, 2016).

[Party affiliation—Gallup poll, 2015]:http://www.gallup.com/poll/188096/democratic-republican-identification-near-historical-lows.aspx (accessed August 18, 2016).

[Wyoming presidential election results]:http://soswy.state.wy.us/information/docs/PresidentialVote.pdf (accessed August 18, 2016).

[History of Wyoming's Governors]:http://soswy.state.wy.us/information/docs/GovernorRoster.pdf (accessed August 18, 2016).

[Presidential elections voter turnout in 2004, 2008 and 2012]:http://bipartisanpolicy.org/library/2012-voter-turnout/ (accessed August 18, 2016).

[2004 Presidential Election public appearances by candidates in battleground states]: Darshan J. Goux and David A. Hopkins *The Empirical Implications of Electoral College Reform (*American Politics Research, 2008) http://greatcommunicatordebate.wikispaces.com/file/view/Electoral+College+Reform.pdf (accessed August 18, 2016)

[2012 campaign advertising]: http://www.washingtonpost.com/wp-srv/special/politics/track-presidential-campaign-ads-2012/ (accessed August 18, 2016).

[Susan Page, USA Today]: http://usatoday30.usatoday.com/news/washington/2002/06-17-bushstates.htm (accessed August 18, 2016).

[Arlen Specter quote]: *The Vanishing Battleground*, NY Times, November 4, 2012 http://www.nytimes.com/2012/11/04/sunday-review/the-vanishing-electoral-battleground.html?pagewanted=all&_r=0 (accessed August 18, 2016).

[No other country uses a system similar to the U.S.]: Steven L. Taylor, Matthew Soberg Shugart, Arend Lijphart, Bernard Grofman, *A Different Democracy: American Government in a 31-Country Perspective* Page 231 (New Haven: Yale University Press, 2014)

[Number of State Constitutional Conventions and Constitutions]: G. Alan Tarr, *Understanding State Constitutions* (Princeton: Princeton University Press, 2000)

[Patrick Henry Quote]: Bill Whitehouse, *Democracy Lost and Regained* (Bangor: Interrogative Imperative Institute, 2009)

[Voting record of the Constitutional Convention]: https://research.archives.gov/id/301680 (accessed August 18, 2016).

[Description of the Constitutional Convention's deliberations over method for selecting the president]: Ray Raphael, *Mr. President: How and Why the Founders Created a Chief Executive* (New York: Alfred A. Knopf, 2012)

[State polls showing support for a national popular vote]: http://www.nationalpopularvote.com/polls#SINCE1944 (accessed August 18, 2016).

[National polls showing support for a national popular vote]: The Washington Post-Kaiser Family Foundation-Harvard University Survey of Political Independents:http://www.washingtonpost.com/wp-srv/politics/interactives/independents/post-kaiser-harvard-topline.pdf (accessed August 18, 2016).

Colorado attempt to reform its awarding of electoral votes]: http://thinkprogress.org/justice/2013/01/25/1497881/electoral-rigging-colorado-2004/ (accessed August 18, 2016).

Pennsylvania attempt to reform its awarding of electoral votes]: http://articles.philly.com/2012-12-11/news/35752061_1_national-popular-vote-electoral-votes-electoral-college-reform (accessed August 18, 2016).

[National Popular Vote Interstate Compact]: http://www.nationalpopularvote.com/ (accessed August 18, 2016).

CHAPTER ELEVEN: FORMER PRESIDENTS, AMERICA'S FUTURE

[Lyndon B. Johnson quote]: Nancy Gibbs, James Duffy, *The Presidents Club* (New York: Simon & Schuster, 2013)

[U.S. population and land area in 1790]: *Historical Statistics of the United States, 1789 – 1945*, Bureau of the Census: http://www2.census.gov/prod2/statcomp/documents/HistoricalStatisticsoftheUnitedStates1789-1945.pdf (accessed August 20, 2016).

[U.S. Gross Domestic Product in 1790]: https://www.measuringworth.com/usgdp/# (accessed August 20, 2016).

[U.S. federal budget in 1790]: https://www.whitehouse.gov/sites/default/files/omb/budget/fy2011/assets/hist.pdf (accessed August 20, 2016).

[U.S. federal workforce]:https://www.opm.gov/policy-data-oversight/data-analysis-documentation/federal-employment-reports/historical-tables/total-government-employment-since-1962/ (accessed August 20, 2016).

[Largest employers in the world]:http://www.forbes.com/sites/niallmccarthy/2015/06/23/the-worlds-biggest-employers-infographic/#77bfc83c51d0 (accessed August 20, 2016).

[2015 Annual Report to Congress on White House Staff]:https://www.whitehouse.gov/briefing-room/disclosures/annual-records/2015 (accessed August 20, 2016).

[Executive Office of the President, 2017 Congressional Budget Submission]: https://www.whitehouse.gov/sites/default/files/docs/fy2017eopbudget finalelectronic.pdf (accessed August 20, 2016).

[Size of presidential staff from George Washington through 1930s]: John P. Burke, *The Institutional Presidency : Organizing and Managing the White House from FDR to Clinton*, 1992 (Baltimore : Johns Hopkins University Press, 2000)

[Former Presidents Act of 1958]: http://www.archives.gov/about/laws/former-presidents.html (accessed August 20, 2016).

[Lifetime Secret Service protection for Presidents]: http://www.usatoday.com/story/theoval/2013/01/10/obama-secret-service-lifetime-protection-bush/1823961/ (accessed August 20, 2016).

Former Presidents Office and Security Costs and Other Information, General Accounting Office, Report to Congress, 2001, http://www.gao.gov/new.items/d01983.pdf (accessed August 20, 2016).

Wendy Ginsberg, *Former Presidents: Pensions, Office Allowances, and Other Federal Benefits*, Congressional Research Service, August 22, 2008:http://fpc.state.gov/documents/organization/109502.pdf (accessed August 20, 2016).

[Annual federal expenses for Presidential libraries]: National Archives and Records Administration, FY 2016 Congressional Justification, February 2, 2016:https://www.archives.gov/about/plans-reports/performance-budget/2016-performance-budget.pdf (accessed August 20, 2016).

[Harry Truman quote]: Nancy Gibbs, James Duffy, *The Presidents Club* (New York: Simon & Schuster, 2013)

[George Washington post-Presidential service as Commander-in-Chief]: http://founders.archives.gov/documents/Hamilton/01-22-02-0002-0002#ARHN-01-22-02-0002-0002-fn-0058 (accessed August 20, 2016).

[Presidential interactions with former presidents, from Truman through today]: Nancy Gibbs, James Duffy, *The Presidents Club* (New York: Simon & Schuster, 2013)

[Presidential luncheon]:http://www.washingtonpost.com/wp-dyn/content/article/2009/01/07/AR2009010700257.html (accessed August 20, 2016).

[Kennedy consultations during Cuban missile crisis]: Max Frankel, *High Noon in the Cold War: Kennedy, Khrushchev, and the Cuban Missile Crisis* (New York: Presidio Press, 2005)

[Doug Brinkley quote]: http://www.cnn.com/2009/POLITICS/01/07/presidents.meeting/ (accessed August 20, 2016).

[Framers of the Constitution deliberations on the structure of the Chief Executive]: Ray Raphael, *Mr. President: How and Why the Founders Created a Chief Executive* (New York: Alfred A. Knopf, 2012)

[George W. Bush approval rating]: http://www.cbsnews.com/news/bushs-final-approval-rating-22-percent/ (accessed August 20, 2016).

[George W. Bush accomplishments with HIV in Africa]: http://abcnews.go.com/blogs/politics/2013/04/george-w-bushs-legacy-on-africa-wins-praise-even-from-foes/ (accessed August 20, 2016).

[George W. Bush accomplishment brokering peace in Sudanese civil war]: http://foreignpolicy.com/2015/02/25/unmade-in-the-usa-south-sudan-bush-obama/ (accessed August 20, 2016).

[Robert Gates]: https://www.washingtonpost.com/lifestyle/style/robert-gates-says-hes-at-peace-but-in-his-new-memoir-his-duty-seems-to-weigh-heavily/2014/01/12/54f1a8b0-7943-11e3-b1c5-739e63e9c9a7_story.html (accessed August 20, 2016).

[Net worth of current and former presidents]:http://247wallst.com/banking-finance/2010/05/17/the-net-worth-of-the-american-presidents-washington-to-obama/4/ (accessed August 20, 2016).

CHAPTER TWELVE: LEADERSHIP IS A TEAM SPORT: BROKERING PEACE IN WASHINGTON

[Voter turnout]: http://www.presidency.ucsb.edu/data/turnout.php (accessed August 25, 2016)

[History of the Annual Messages and State of the Union addresses]: http://history.house.gov/Institution/SOTU/List/ (accessed August 6, 2016); http://www.presidency.ucsb.edu/sou.php (accessed August 20, 2016)

[History of presidential involvement in legislation]: http://www.heritage.org/constitution/#!/articles/2/essays/95/recomm endations-clause (accessed July 30, 2016).

[Jefferson rejection of oral Annual Message to Congress]: https://fas.org/sgp/crs/misc/R40132.pdf (accessed August 20, 2016)

[Woodrow Wilson's address to Congress]: http://history.house.gov/Blog/2013/January/01-31-Wilson_Message/ (accessed September 19, 2016)

[Woodrow Wilson, *Congressional Government: A Study in American Politics*]: https://archive.org/stream/congressionalgov00wilsa#page/n357/mode /2up (accessed September 19, 2016)

James Pfiffner, *The Modern Presidency* (New York: St. Martin's Press, 1994).

[USS Sequoia]: http://www.sequoiayacht.com/index.htm.

[Ronald Reagan]: http://www.usnews.com/news/articles/2004/06/21/ronald-reagan-tip-oneill-and-the-clash-of-the-titans (accessed August 6, 2016).

[No Labels]:https://www.nolabels.org/regular-meetings-between-the-president-and-congressional-leadership/ (accessed August 6, 2016).

[Obama consideration of Camp David retreat with Republicans in 2010]: http://thehill.com/homenews/campaign/131143-obama-floats-camp-david-retreat-with-gop-at-white-house-meeting (accessed August 21, 2016)

[Obama proposal for Camp David retreat following 2012 elections]: http://www.newsmax.com/Newsfront/Camp-David-talks-book/2013/11/04/id/534752/#ixzz3O3RqrtSP (accessed August 21, 2016)

[Boehner and Pelosi rejecting the Camp David retreat]: http://www.reuters.com/article/us-usa-debt-campdavid-idUSTRE76D3A720110714 (accessed August 21, 2016)

CHAPTER THIRTEEN: WILD CARD

[Congressional Caucuses]: https://cha.house.gov/sites/republicans.cha.house.gov/files/documents /114CMOList%287.18.16%29.pdf (accessed August 6, 2016).

APPENDIX

[Twelfth Amendment]: http://constitutioncenter.org/interactive-constitution/amendments/amendment-xii (accessed August 27, 2016)

[Seventeenth Amendment]:
http://mason.gmu.edu/~tzywick2/Cleveland%20State%20Senators.pdf;
http://www.senate.gov/artandhistory/history/common/generic/SeventeenthAmendment.htm (accessed August 27, 2016)

[Twenty Second Amendment]: Stephen W. Stathis, *The Twenty-Second Amendment: A Practical Remedy Or Partisan Maneuver?* (Constitutional Commentary, Volume 7:61)
https://conservancy.umn.edu/bitstream/handle/11299/165281/07_01_Stathis.pdf?sequence=1&isAllowed=y (accessed August 27, 2016)

94179915R00113

Made in the USA
Columbia, SC
23 April 2018

ABOUT THE AUTHOR

Jeff Edelstein is a public policy mediator who has worked for over twenty years helping local, state and federal government entities solve problems, make decisions, and resolve conflict. His work has focused in the environmental arena, in which he has helped resolve conflict and build consensus on a wide variety of contentious issues, including U.S. coastal management, natural gas drilling in the Greater Yellowstone Ecosystem, federal forest management legislation, Superfund hazardous waste cleanup in New York City, Clean Water Act and Safe Drinking Water Act litigation, and Tar Sands pipeline regulation. More information is available at www.jeffedelstein.com or www.fromoathtoaction.com.